METAMORPHOSIS

METAMORPHOSIS

An Anthology of Poetry & Prose

LUW PRESS

METAMORPHOSIS
An Anthology of Poetry & Prose

Copyright © 2019 LUW Press

ISBN: 978-0-9882367-7-6

Cover design by Lauren Makena

"Gratitude bestows reverence, allowing us to encounter everyday epiphanies, those transcendent moments of awe that change forever how we experience life and the world."

- John Milton

Contents

Summer Sandcastles
C. H. Lindsay

Kraken waves
   batter
      castle walls,
         drag souvenirs
      to murky lairs.

Leviathan water
   slithers
      through passages
         searching out
      hidden occupants.

Poseidon surge
   roars,
      withdraws,
         trails desolation
      in shadowed wake.

Colossus foot
   smashes
      sodden remains,
         demolishes
      civilization.

Charybdis sea
   swallows
      a day of Creation,
         as childish laughter
      dances through air.

A Friend in Need
Caryn Larrinaga

THE IMPOSSIBILITY exhausted me. She couldn't be there. But in defiance of all logic, Emily lurked in the corner of the classroom, trying to catch my eye from behind Dr. Radcliffe's desk. It took effort to ignore her, to block out the stare that burned into my forehead in a way it had never done while she was still awake. I refused to look, choosing instead to focus on the half-empty can of Super Energy Blast at the edge of my desk. "She's not here," I muttered to the can. "She's not here."

The repeated mantra didn't do any good. Emily remained, her brown eyes wide and unblinking, same as she'd done for the past week. No matter where I was, no matter what time of day . . . if I got tired enough, she'd be there. Chugging energy drinks bought me a couple sleepless days and nights of peace, but the caffeine crash loomed right around the corner. The fatigue pressed down on me like a weight— God, I wanted to close my eyes. Close them for a minute and rest . . .

"Still with us, Annie?"

My eyelids snapped open at the sound of Dr. Radcliffe's voice. She frowned at me from beside the blackboard.

"Sorry." I cleared my throat and stretched in my seat, then grabbed my pen and tried to copy the chart Dr. Radcliffe had written while I'd been dozing. I welcomed the distraction from Emily's gaze, and I took care to write my notes, including more details than I'd ever done in four years of college.

"As you can see, the grading is very straightforward. If you get your senior projects in on time, follow the formatting guidelines, and stay on topic, there's no reason you won't pass. See me during my office hours if you have additional questions. Class dismissed."

There was a loud scraping of chairs as the other students in my advisory group packed up their things and left the classroom. I stuffed my notebook into my messenger bag, hoping to sneak out while Dr. Radcliffe erased the board, but when I raised my head, she was already standing at my desk.

"Do you have a minute?" she asked.

"Sure." I tried to make it sound casual, like I had no idea what she wanted to talk to me about, but the spike in my voice betrayed me.

Dr. Radcliffe half-sat on the desk across from mine and looked at me for a few silent moments. I ran my hands over my head and straightened my ponytail, hoping I didn't look as disheveled as I felt. I showered at least twice a day in my bid to stay awake, but my old routine of straightening my hair and picking fun, layered outfits had long since fallen to the wayside in favor of hair ties and whatever T-shirt smelled cleanest.

At last she spoke, tilting her head toward my energy drink. "Doesn't seem to be working."

"No, not really."

"Listen, I know you've got a lot of finals to study for. And I can't imagine what you must be going through since Emily . . ." She trailed off and pursed her lips. "Well, I'm extending the deadline on your senior project. Why don't you take summer semester to wrap it up?"

I shook my head. "You don't need to do that for me. I'm fine."

"I really think you should. It could make—"

"No." The booming volume of my voice surprised me. I lowered it to explain myself. "I appreciate your concern, but I don't want to delay my graduation."

Another semester here would do me in. I couldn't take the stares from my classmates, the pity from my professors. Emily was the one who'd gotten sick, not me. She was the one who wouldn't wake up. But nobody was trying to help her; they all seemed focused on me.

I didn't get it. I wasn't Emily's only roommate. I wasn't even the one who'd found her and called the paramedics. I wondered if Zuri's professors offered to extend deadlines or waive assignments. Knowing Zuri, probably not.

"I'll have my project to you next week," I said. "Same as everybody else."

I zipped my backpack and stood. I felt Dr. Radcliffe's eyes following me out of the classroom, but I didn't turn around. Her gaze was a hell of a lot easier to ignore than Emily's.

A vicious funk greeted me when I opened the door to our apartment. I glanced at the Jenga tower of dishes piled in the sink, thought about washing them, and opted to open a window and air the place out instead. Cleaning was one of many things I'd avoided since the paramedics had wheeled Emily away, and Zuri was too busy with Student Council activities to care that I wasn't pulling my weight. That, or maybe she took the same kind of pity on me as everyone else and just wasn't bitching at me about it.

I shoved an empty pizza box off the couch and stretched out across the soft cushions. It was easier to ignore Emily out here than in our bedroom. In there, she stared at me from the hundreds of selfies and group photos we'd taken together over the last four years. Out here, she only stared at me from the corner where Zuri kept her yoga mat.

"Hey, Emily," I told her. "I know you're a figment of my imagination, but I'd still appreciate it if you'd let me squeeze in a nap before chem lab."

She mouthed something in return, but I couldn't hear it. I could never hear it. The words were probably random song lyrics or something else my brain was too worn-out to process in any healthy way. Maybe after graduation, when there was more space in my head, I'd finally figure it out.

A light hum filled my ears. I felt the forceful tug of sleep on my eyelids. My body, impatient for rest—deep, quality rest—tugged me deeper into the cushions. I closed my eyes and hovered briefly on the edge between consciousness and nothingness.

"Annie!"

Emily's voice slapped the buzz of sleepiness from my mind. It'd been exactly twenty-eight days since I'd last heard it. When I opened my eyes, she wasn't skulking in the corner anymore. She kneeled beside the couch, eyes frantic and cheeks flushed.

I scrambled to sit up and backed away from her, pulling my knees to my chest and trying to retreat as far back into the cushions as possible. I trained my eyes on the ceiling fan and whispered my mantra, "She's not here. She's not here."

"Annie, I'm here!"

"She's not here. Not here. Not here." I shook my head and pinched my arms and legs. "I'm dreaming. Wake up!"

"Look at me, Nan!"

I hated that nickname. Emily only used it when she was trying to nettle me. Out of sheer reflex, I turned my head and shot her a glare. Her eyes went wide, and words—finally audible after so long—spilled out of her mouth at light speed.

"Listen! You're awake, and I'm here!" She glanced down at her chest, which was translucent enough that I could see the pile of unwashed clothes behind her. "Or I guess part of me is. My body's still in the hospital. But I hate it there, Annie! Please, help me come home!"

I stared at her, really looking for the first time in weeks. "Is it really you?"

She tried to grab for my hand, but she passed right through my body. "Yes, it's me. I've been trying to talk to you for days." A tear rolled down her cheek. "I can't believe you can actually hear me."

My brain imitated my car engine in the dead of winter, half starting and then choking out. Again and again I turned the keys, trying to process what the hell was going on here. Emily, in our living room, talking to me . . . But it couldn't be real. She couldn't be real. I'd seen her the day before in her hospital room, tubes and wires coming out of her throat and arms. She'd been skinnier there, thinner than she looked now, with limp, stringy hair and skin the color of ash.

"You're not here," I whispered. "You're in a coma. You're sick—"

"I'm not sick!" She reached for me again, then seemed to remember that she couldn't touch me and dragged her hand down her face instead. "That's why I need to get out of there. The doctors will *never* be able to help me. It's not an infection or a fever."

I'd never seen that desperate look in her eyes before. Even when she'd been stressed or sad, there'd always been a light, a hint of a smile waiting to be coaxed out by a good joke. I'd never imagined she could look so frightened.

My chest constricted. This was something I *hadn't* imagined. This was real. Emily—my best friend, my confidante, the person who'd gotten me through every failed test and bad breakup—sat here, translucent, asking for my help.

I straightened up. "Okay. If you're not sick, why are you in a coma?"

"It was a demon."

"A demon?"

Under different circumstances, I would've laughed. On a normal day, Emily might have been rehearsing for an audition or playing a practical joke. But I didn't think Emily would've stalked me like a living ghost for the past week just to prank me, so I had to take anything she told me at face value.

Which means, I realized, *that she's talking about an honest-to-God actual demon.*

I struggled for words. "I don't ... I don't know how I can help with that."

Emily's face was still flushed, but now that I'd agreed she was, in fact, somehow visiting me from the confines of her hospital bed, her pupils had grown still, and she looked less like a desperate addict jonesing for her next fix.

"There's a book in my desk," she said. "Get it. The last page has everything you need to know."

"Okay, I'll be right back."

As much as I loved Emily, my self-preservation instincts wouldn't let me stand up, walk by her, and then turn my back to her to go down the hall. Instead, I climbed over the back of the couch, like a weirdo, and shuffled out of the room in reverse, not turning around until I entered our bedroom and closed the door.

As I'd expected, the wall of selfies assaulted me. I froze, staring at them. Emily was everywhere—smiling, laughing, sharing her brilliant light with the world. I didn't want that light to go out forever. I balled my hands into fists and marched across the room, letting hundreds of pairs of brown eyes follow me to Emily's desk. I hadn't touched so much as a pencil on it since she'd gotten sick—no, since she'd been *taken*—but now I rifled through every stack of paper, upended every drawer in search of whatever book she'd been talking about. The only books I'd found were textbooks, and the last pages of those were appendixes and glossaries. Nothing in them suggested "Hey, I can help with this demon problem."

"Dammit!" I banged my fists on the desk, and something landed on my foot—a small, brown book that barely filled my hand when I picked it up. I ran my thumb down the empty spine; there was no title, no markings at all. Just smooth, faded leather. I pulled back on the pages and let them flip past me. Neat, cramped handwriting filled each page.

"A journal," I muttered.

I knew it wasn't Emily's. She always said journaling was too much work, but she kept a diary in her own way. She had accounts on every kind of social media and busily photographed and posted the most mundane details of her daily life, especially if she encountered a stray animal or a particularly cute cup of coffee. Plus, her handwriting was a loopy, messy half cursive that was a headache to read. Whoever wrote this clearly took extra effort to make sure it was legible. It looked like it could have been typed, except for variations in the print size and the occasional inkblot.

The book was short, and it didn't take long to flip to the end. A perfect circle filled with odd shapes and symbols took up the entire last page. Most of it didn't make any sense to me, but a few looked like stick figures and stars. Below the circle, there was a drawing of a single lit candle, beside which were thick, block letters spelling: TRANSIET IN TENEBRAE.

Still examining that final page, I opened the bedroom door and went back to the couch.

"Where the hell did you get this?" I asked.

There was no answer, and Emily was gone when I raised my head. I sighed. Searching her desk had gotten me so keyed up, I could've run a marathon. I was more awake than I'd been in almost a month, and she only appeared when I was beat. I'd have to wait until the high of excitement wore off.

The stink from the kitchen sink wafted over to me, pulled by the breeze from the open window.

"Might as well wear myself out," I muttered, turning on the faucet.

"This is a nice surprise." Zuri stood in the doorway with her hands on her hips and surveyed the apartment. "No dishes in the sink *and* I can actually see the floor?"

"I aim to please." I lay stretched out on the sofa, taking up all three cushions beneath my softest fleece blanket. I'd put the little brown book in my pillowcase for safekeeping. I could feel the ridge of it through the stuffing in my pillow.

She crossed the room to perch on the arm of the couch, took the mug out of my hand, and sniffed it. "Chamomile? Did you finally sell your stock in Super Energy Blast?"

"Just trying to relax." In truth, I was trying to bring myself back to the brink of falling asleep. The tea, the blanket, the home shopping channel that played on the TV—they were all part of a strategy that didn't seem to be working. Had I known this whole time that wanting to fall asleep was the secret to staying awake, I would've saved a fortune on energy drinks.

"I'm glad." Zuri's voice was soft, and she reached down to squeeze my foot. "I haven't wanted to say anything, but I've been worried about you."

I clenched my jaw and said nothing, despite the torrent of angry responses that flooded my mind. Zuri, like everyone else, was more worried about me than Emily. Like everyone else, she professed concern but didn't do much more than talk about it. But if I told her how I felt, we'd get into an argument, and the adrenaline would keep me awake. So I lay there, staring at a spinning silver bracelet on the television screen, and kept quiet.

She sighed and set the mug down on the coffee table. "I know you think it's pity or something, but it's not. I miss you, Annie. You've been different since Emily got sick."

"She didn't get sick." I couldn't help it; the words leaped from my mouth. "She was taken."

"What are you talking about?"

"Nothing."

She slid off the armrest and rounded the couch to kneel in front of me. Her eyebrows were drawn together so tightly that, for a second, I thought she was angry. But when she spoke, her voice was as gentle as always.

"Okay, tough talk time," she said. "I've been trying to figure out how to have this conversation with you for weeks, but I couldn't find the right words. Well, screw the right words. Annie, you need help."

I narrowed my eyes at her. "Help?"

"You're not processing what happened to Emily in a healthy way. There are grief counselors—"

"Grief? She's not dead!"

"Well, she might as well be!" For the first time in the four years I'd known her, Zuri raised her voice to a near shriek. She grabbed one of my hands in both of her own, and her eyes filled with tears. "Don't you get it? She's probably never going to wake up. Every day she's in that coma, it's less likely she'll come back to us. We have to let go."

I yanked my hand out of her grasp. "Let go? How can you say that? She's our friend!"

"She *was* our friend. That's what I'm saying. Since the moment the paramedics wheeled her out of here, she's been gone. Can't you feel it?"

"Feel what?"

"She used to fill this whole place with light and energy." Zuri looked around the room with flat, sad eyes. "I can't feel her here anymore."

"Maybe you can't, but I can. I've seen her." Would she believe me if I told her Emily had been kneeling in exactly the spot Zuri now sat, just hours earlier? "I've talked to her."

"Oh, Annie." She sat back on her heels and let her hands fall into her lap. "Why didn't you tell me it'd gotten this bad?"

"When could I have told you? You're never home."

She pursed her lips. For a minute, I thought it was over, that I'd won this argument. It was a good thing too, because I was starting to shake and I knew I'd already undone all the work I'd put into relaxing.

"I'm sorry," she said. "It's hard, being home. You weren't here when I found her. You get to remember her the way she was at breakfast, happy and bubbly. But every time I walk into this room, I see it all over again. The furniture was everywhere—even the rug was rumpled up by the TV—and she was just lying there." She pointed to the space in front of the fireplace. "It looked like she was sleeping, but when I checked for her pulse, there wasn't one. I thought she was dead. I can't remember calling 911, but I remember sitting there with her cold, still hand in mine."

I stared at her. She'd never talked about it before, not like this. To be honest, I hadn't been able to bring myself to ask. I didn't want to think about it. It was bad enough that Emily was unconscious in a hospital bed without dwelling on what put her there.

Zuri was right: I was lucky. I didn't envy that memory. Maybe Emily was lucky too—lucky I wasn't there and wasn't haunted by what I'd seen. I was able to be here, to see her.

I considered telling Zuri what I'd found and including her in the plan to bring Emily back, but her red-rimmed eyes and slumped shoulders made me suspect she needed sleep even more than I did. Guilt twisted in my stomach. I'd been so wrapped up in my own sadness that I hadn't been paying attention to hers.

"Can I get you anything?" I asked. "Want some of this tea?"

"There's only one thing I want," she said. "I want you to get help. I want you to be able to move on."

"Okay," I said. Compared to what I faced with Emily, Zuri's request was nothing. "I'm guessing you already have the name of somebody you want me to see, right? I'll call them tomorrow and make an appointment."

Zuri's eyes widened. "Really?"

"Really."

She jumped forward, pulled me into a tight hug, and whispered in my ear, "Thank you."

"Why don't you go lie down or something?"

She pulled away from me and shook her head. "I've got a planning meeting for the graduation concert. It's going to be really nice. They're going to dedicate a song to Emily." She ran the middle finger of each hand under her eyes, brushing away gray lines of running mascara. "I'm going to splash some water on my face and head back to campus."

While she cleaned up in the bathroom, I snuggled back down into the blanket and yawned. If she was that happy getting me to agree to see a counselor, I couldn't wait to see her face when Emily woke up.

After Zuri left and the sun began to set, I felt the familiar weight of sleepiness pressing down on me. I blinked, and when I opened my eyes, Emily stood in front of the fireplace. She was more translucent than before, and I could see every detail of the picture frames behind her.

"I found the book," I told her.

Her eyes lit up. "I knew you would."

I sat up and leaned forward with my elbows on my knees. "So how does this work? I read the words and you wake up?"

She shook her head. "I wish it were that easy. You need to stand in the circle, hold the candle, and speak the words. That will connect us, so you can pull me out of the darkness."

"The darkness?"

"I don't know how else to describe it. It's where he's keeping me. It's so dark here, so empty. I want to come home!"

I wanted to jump up and hug her, then remembered I couldn't. "It's okay, Em. I'm coming for you."

"Please hurry." Her form flickered, fading like a candle about to go out. "It's been nearly a month. I don't have much longer."

"What happens when—"

She disappeared before I could finish my question.

"Shit!"

I dived to the side and retrieved the book from my pillowcase. The circle filled with odd symbols waited for me on the last page, but it was barely four inches tall. Emily said I should stand inside it. I needed to draw a much larger version, plus find a candle somewhere.

Swearing under my breath, I dashed into the kitchen and started rummaging through our junk drawer. There, among the rubber bands and spare charging cables, I found a candle shaped like the number two, left over from Emily's twenty-second birthday a few months before, along with a small box of matches.

"Aha!"

At the back of the drawer, my hand closed around a cold metal tube. It was a giant, black magic marker, the kind Zuri used to make posters for Student Council events. I had everything I needed, except somewhere to draw the circle.

I crossed back into the living room, twisting the marker between my fingers and racking my brain for something I could draw on. Regular paper was too small. Zuri might have some poster board in her room, or I could check the dumpster for an old cardboard box. Or to hell with it, I could draw on the floor. We'd lose our deposit when we moved out after graduation ... Maybe I could cover it with the rug.

It wasn't even a rug, really. It was a thin piece of carpet the previous tenants left behind. I lifted the edge and saw a curved line, delicately carved into the scuffed hardwood beneath the rug.

It looked like a piece of a circle.

I dropped the corner back down with a slap, dragged the coffee table out of the way, and pulled the rug over the back of the couch to fully expose the floor. I was right; it was a circle. The carving was faded, but some parts stood out clearly, especially in the lower-traffic areas like where the coffee table normally sat. There, I could easily make out a figure encased in a star that matched the last page in Emily's book.

Did she draw this? I bent down and ran my thumb along the edge of the design, feeling the smoothness of the floor that was barely marred by the shallow carving. It seemed old, like years of feet walking on top of it had sanded down the ridges and made the lines less severe. No, she hadn't carved it, but maybe she used it. I stood and walked forward, wondering how many of her steps I was retracing.

The instant my feet hit the center of the circle, the little hairs on the back of my neck twitched. I was close to something powerful. I suddenly wanted to leave the apartment, find Zuri at her meeting, and never return. I certainly didn't want to light the candle that threatened to slip out of my sweaty fingers, and the thought of speaking those foreign words made bile rise up in my throat. But when I closed my eyes, I saw Emily's fading figure and heard her plea for help.

She was depending on me. She'd stood by me for four years—four years of roller-coaster emotions, insane workloads, and living on a shoestring in the hopes that we'd have a better future. Now all she needed from me was one thing—one small thing, really: to swallow my fear and stick to the plan—so she could have that future.

I gulped down the stomach acid, struck a match, and lit the candle. Holding it above my head, I spoke the words from the book, "Transiet in tenebrae." When my mouth closed over the final syllable, the candle blew out and the lights went dark above me. The room was lit only by the full moon shining through the open window. As I blinked, it began to fade until I stood in a blackness so complete that I couldn't make out my own hand in front of my face.

"Emily?" I whispered. My voice was strangely muffled, as though I were talking through a pillow. "Are you here?"

No reply. I wanted to vomit, faint, and run away all at the same time. Just as I was deciding that option number two was the best choice out of those three, a glowing orb appeared in my peripheral vision. It was moving, growing larger ... or coming closer. It was hard to tell which. Soon, the light of the orb filled my entire field of vision, and what I saw inside made my heart swell.

"Emily!"

She lay on the floor of the orb, curled up in the fetal position. Unlike when she'd appeared to me earlier that day, this version of her looked like the one that lay in the hospital bed: thin, wasted, her normally curly hair matted against her forehead.

"Emily!" I shouted again. "I'm here!"

She opened her eyes and lifted her head, squinting at me from inside the glowing ball. "Annie? Is that you?"

"Come on," I told her. "I'm taking you home."

I reached forward to grab her hand and yank her out of her prison. As my fingers neared the edge of the glowing light, Emily's eyes widened. "No!" she shrieked.

But it was too late to stop my momentum. I touched the orb and it exploded, blinding me with a flash of lightning and deafening me with a roar of thunder. My legs buckled beneath me, and I let out a cry of pain, echoed by Emily's screaming. The light faded … faded … faded … into nothing.

Emily didn't have long. Soon, I knew, she'd become like the dozens of other husks in the orb with us. They'd been people, once. Now they looked like set pieces from a horror film about a mummy's tomb.

I'd spent days pounding at the glowing haze that surrounded us. It looked like little more than smoke, but was as solid as steel. I was too weak for that now, too weak to fight. Instead, I sat on the floor of the orb and stroked Emily's hair, listening to her ragged breathing. Through the haze, I could make out Zuri sitting on the couch in our living room. She hugged a pillow to her chest and cried, her tears spilling onto my fleece blanket. My heart ached for her, for all of us, but there was nothing I could do. The demon had already taken my form, following Zuri and haunting her at her most exhausted. Soon enough, she'd find the book, and she'd already seen the carving. Twice.

Emily was too weak to answer my questions, and I wondered what form the demon had taken to lure her here. Knowing her, I guessed it could've been anything from a scared puppy to a perfect stranger who needed help. No wonder she'd been the first to go.

And soon, she really would be gone. I'd sit here, alone, until Zuri fell for the demon's tricks. At least then, I'd have someone to stroke my hair while I withered away in the darkness.

Straining to Hear
Lorraine Jeffery

I knew crowded apartments,
others' crying babies,
cooking's oily smell,
thud of overhead footsteps,
blaring horns, the static
of traffic, I no longer heard.

He dreamed of large far away
expanses, a new life,
so I promised. I didn't
know of flat
dead mesas,
never-ending wind
from the bellows of hell,
scraggly greasewood's needles,
rabbit brush browning
in hot red sand,
rock-hard clay, deadly alkali,
streams vanishing in July,
dams breaking and draining.

I never imagined straining
to hear human voices in the wind.

I knead the small of my back,
watch him survey his acres
in a stained shirt, as new life
grows in my belly, wondering
if this summer will bake the crops,
if the dam will hold—
if a baby can suck life
from a father's dream.

Regret
Keri Montgomery

IT WASN'T UNTIL she slipped the sleeping powder into Jeremiah's drink that Nora experienced a twinge of regret. At that point, *regret* was a relative term. She could also say that she regretted the nature of their relationship—regretted allowing herself to be trapped and helpless in such a life. By comparison, the slight remorse she felt for drugging him was easier to handle.

Nora waited as his lips pressed against the glass, her husband tilting back and ingesting innocent sips of red wine as if mere alcohol were the only potent substance entering his body. Yes, he would hate her after waking from a heavy sleep, but Jeremiah's hate was worth enduring if it meant a few peaceful hours away from him.

"How is your roast?" she asked, examining his breathing pattern.

"It's dry," he said. "But you're getting better at the gravy. Almost like my mother's. Well, closer anyway." He sliced the meat with his steak knife.

She bit her bottom lip. "I'm planning a trip to the grocery store tomorrow. You never know when we'll need more cold medicine. Feeling ill can happen fast."

He wrinkled his nose, staring at the wine bottle. "Where did this come from?" he asked. "I don't recognize the label."

"Um, the bottle's a thank you gift from the new neighbors across the street. The woman said her uncle owns a winery in northern California. They have tons of the stuff." Nora straightened the cloth napkin on her lap, all the while eyeing the way her husband shifted in his chair.

"A thank you?" Jeremiah looked up, fixing on her, his stare deep. "For what?"

"I baked them a lemon cake as a welcome-to-the-neighborhood gesture."

"How long did you visit?" He wiped away the fresh beads of sweat lining his forehead and unknowingly plastered strands of moist blonde hair against his temples.

She didn't reply to his question. The words caught in her throat.

"Nora, I don't want you baking things for the neighbors. We don't know anything about them. And why do you want go to the store? We talked about this. You can order everything we need online. Have it delivered. There's no reason for you to leave the house. Ever."

"The woman seems nice," she said. "Her name is Sylvie. They moved in on Saturday. I was being welcoming. Besides, we live in a cul-de-sac. I hardly left our yard to meet her."

He stared at Nora, his lips tightening and his posture hunching a few inches closer to the table. "But you know I don't approve of—"

"Jeremiah—" Nora recoiled, realizing her tone was getting too impatient. She forced her own posture to relax, to appear casual. "Alright … I get it."

"Do you?" Jeremiah placed his napkin alongside his dinner plate. His fingers dragged against the tablecloth before returning to his glass. He finished the wine quickly, the last bit in a single gulp. "So, what exactly did you and the neighbor talk about?"

"Things. The neighborhood mostly. Small talk. It was harmless. Only lasted a minute, maybe less."

"Anything else?" he asked, loosening his tie and slouching forward a few more inches in his chair. His breathing sounded faint.

"Sweetheart," she said, steadying her voice. "You're tired. Was work hard today? Maybe you should rest on the couch for a while."

"Nora, please." His words began to slur together. "Working in my home office isn't exactly a sweatshop. It's not exhausting. I'm fine.

32

And don't change the subject. No befriending anyone. Do you understand me? I don't want you talking to the neighbors."

She hesitated for a moment, staring down at her plate of barely-touched dry roast and the not-quite-his-mother's gravy. "Okay. You're right. You're always right. I won't talk to Sylvie anymore. Honey, please go lie down. Rest."

"I said I'm fine."

"You need to lie down. Please, dear." She stood from the table while reaching for his plate. "Go to the couch. I'll bring you a blanket right after I put your dinner in the fridge."

Jeremiah stood to his feet. He staggered forward and braced one hand against the dining room wall, his head tilting more toward the floor with each step.

"Okay, I guess," he said. "I do feel a little … *off*."

Nora hurried into the kitchen and shoved the entire plate into the refrigerator. She dismissed the normal practice of covering the leftovers with plastic wrap, knowing her husband wouldn't have much of an appetite when he awoke in eight hours. He'd feel nauseated. The food would go to waste either way. It always did. As she turned, Nora heard a thump on the living room carpet. She ran through the hallway and found Jeremiah lying chest-down in front of the couch, his arms sprawled out as if he'd tried to catch himself.

She checked his pulse first and placed her hand near Jeremiah's mouth to examine his breathing. He exhaled a soft breath against her wrist, the warm air forcing an involuntary tingle along her skin. Just what she wanted. Relief washed over her.

Nora wrapped her arms around Jeremiah's chest and used every ounce of strength to drag his body onto the couch. She flopped his feet onto the cushions, removed his shoes, and finished loosening the tie from around his neck. With any luck, he wouldn't question sleeping all night on the sofa, but Nora knew better. Later she'd feed him a lie. Something about being ill.

After stretching a blanket over his body, Nora stared down at her husband's face. A calm, drug-induced slumber replaced Jeremiah's usual stern expression. She gritted her teeth, struggling to remember the last time she slept that peacefully. Her own nights were filled with nightmares.

"Sweet dreams, Jeremiah." She hurried to their linen closet and pulled out a shoebox stashed behind a pile of decorative throw pillows. In haste, she riffled through the contents of the box—a wallet filled with four thousand dollars in cash, ID cards, a bottle of crushable sleeping pills, and one generic prepaid cell phone. Nora gripped the phone in her hand, cradling it against her chest, and set the box on the carpet. For a moment, she contemplated getting the car keys, but decided against the notion. The sedan was a recent purchase, and Jeremiah knew the mileage.

Instead, Nora headed for the front door. She unlocked the deadbolt, the chain, the keyed doorknob, and punched in the code to disarm the home-security motion sensor, all the while her heart pounded as she freed herself. Instant cool evening air sucked into her lungs and flushed against her skin.

Nora ran for sidewalk, scanning along the quiet, suburban cul-de-sac, and found the live view looked just as it always did from her locked window—picturesque in every sense of the word.

When she reached the end of the grass, Nora paused and stared down at her feet. Setting sunlight formed a golden glow on her house slippers, and warm colors of orange and pink stretched up her body. Nora breathed in deeply, and then exhaled with force as if the action would somehow release her worries into the air. She sucked in freedom again and again, each time wishing the heaviness would leave her stomach.

But it didn't. No matter how sweet freedom tasted, it was poisoned. Just like the wine.

Nora slumped down on the curb and dialed a memorized number into the cell phone.

"Hello?" a woman answered.

"Mom, it's me," Nora said, barely getting out the words.

"Oh, honey. You sound upset. What's wrong?"

"I ... I ... don't know if I can do this anymore ... Jeremiah and I are ..."

"Honey," her mother interrupted. "We've been over this before. This is your life now. As much as I love you and want things to be easier, you can't call me and expect a rescue. That's not how it works."

Nora swallowed hard.

"Honey, you know I'm right," her mother said. "You just shouldn't call me like this. I wish things were different."

Nora nodded, her expression tightening and tears welling up in her eyes. "Yes. I know. I have to stay."

"Okay. Good. But since you've already made the call, how long can you talk? Is Jeremiah—"

A shuffle of footsteps broke Nora's focus. She glanced up to find the new neighbor, Sylvie, walking toward her across the cul-de-sac. The woman had a pleasant smile on her face and held out a plate of cookies.

"Are you alright?" Sylvie asked.

Nora fought to control her breathing, eyeing the woman's kind face and trying to decide what to do. Jeremiah's words echoed over and over in her head: *I don't want you talking to the neighbors.*

"Yes, hang on." Nora tilted away, wiped the tears from her cheeks, and spoke into the phone. "I need to go, Mom. I'll call later if I can."

"Okay, honey. I love you," her mother said before hanging up.

Sylvie handed Nora the plate of cookies. "Nice night. I thought I'd bring over a treat. The lemon cake was delicious. I hope your husband liked the wine."

Nora nodded. She stood from the curb and slid the cell phone into her pocket. "He did. Thank you, Sylvie."

"So, Nora," she said, stepping closer. "I hope we can be friends. Moving into a new place is so hard. I hate not knowing anyone."

"Me too."

"Have you lived here long?" Sylvie motioned toward the house.

"Not too long," Nora said. A surge of worry washed over her, realizing that she'd left the front door wide open. She sidestepped to block the line-of-sight to where Jeremiah lay fully visible on the couch. "It's been a nice place to live."

"Good. But still …" Sylvie smiled wide. "This is my first time living outside of California. Maybe you can give me some advice about getting used to a new place. Must be hard living so far from your family. They are in Illinois, didn't you say?"

Nora absentmindedly nodded.

Then she paused. A cold chill ran along her skin. "Actually, I didn't say."

Sylvie titled her head. "Oh, I think you did. If not, my mistake."

35

Nora's mind raced as she studied the woman's plastered smile. Had she said Illinois? No, she knew better than to make that mistake. "Well, I've gotta go. It's getting late. Thanks for the cookies. We will, uh, get together for lunch or something. Sometime or … I gotta go."

"Sounds perfect."

Nora retreated onto the grass. She headed for the house, all the while fighting off the impulse to run. When she stepped inside, she closed the door and bolted the locks. All of them. Her fingers shook as she armed the home-security system.

"Jeremiah." She tossed the cookie plate onto the living room carpet. "Wake up."

He didn't stir.

"Please, Jeremiah!" Nora shook his shoulders. How could she have been so stupid? How could she have overdosed him on crushed sleeping pills?

The doorbell chimed.

Nora flipped around and stared at the wooden door, then at the closed curtains over the front window. Her limbs flopped like noodles, and her brain seemed to stop short.

The bell rang again.

She crept to the peephole and squinted at the visitor. The image looked distorted—a twisted version of a woman with a plastered smile.

"Nora!" The woman's muffled voice seeped through the wood. "I forgot to ask what day you'd like to have lunch. Do you have a minute to chat?"

The woman touched the bell a third time, pressing it hard so the sound lingered in an electric buzzing.

Nora jolted. She threw her arms around Jeremiah's torso, using momentum to roll him from the couch and into a heap on the carpet. Crumbled cookie bits stuck to the sweat on his face.

"Please, wake up!" she whispered directly into his ear and shook him again without getting a response. "Please!"

A fist knocked on the outside door. "Nora?"

Nora grasped Jeremiah under the arms and dragged his body away from the couch. They nearly made it into the hallway before she collapsed to her knees in exhaustion and panic.

Footsteps shifted outside, then crunched on the wood chips in the flowerbed.

Nora covered her mouth.

A dark shape, silhouetted against the setting sunlight, pressed against glass. The woman held still, attempting the peer through the slit between the curtains.

Nora bit down on her scream. She tried to remember where Jeremiah kept the car keys, and struggled with how in the world she could get his body, herself, and the shoebox into the sedan without making any noise in the garage.

"Wake up! Now!" she pleaded into her husband's ear.

He groaned.

"Please, Jeremiah. I can't do this without you." She pulled the cell phone from her pocket and dialed the only other number she had memorized—this one not listed.

It rang once. "U.S. Marshals' field office. Secure line. Number please," an operator said.

"Witness protection 017496," she whispered.

"Confirmed. What's the problem?"

"There's a woman outside my door. She isn't leaving."

"Do you recognize her?"

"No, but she has to be one of them! She knew what state I'm from."

The operator typed on her keyboard. "Can you get out of the house and reach the secure location for pick up?"

"No. I can't," Nora said. "Send someone!"

"We are contacting local authorities and sending marshals right now. Stay on the phone with me."

Nora nodded, forgetting the operator couldn't see her motion.

The front doorknob rattled quickly and with force, as if the woman was testing the locks. Then Nora heard the distinct clinking of two metal picks in the keyhole.

"Hurry," she whispered into the phone. Nora stared down at Jeremiah, at his peaceful and innocent face, and allowed her raw emotions to completely take over. She couldn't let it end like this. Not after all Jeremiah had done to protect her. Nora gripped his torso and dragged him down the hallway. As she rounded the corner into the kitchen, wood cracked in the front room and the frame and door chain snap loose. A second later the home alarm pierced her eardrums.

Nora reached for the nearest weapon, a gravy-covered steak knife from dinner, and stepped over Jeremiah's body—placing herself between him and the hallway.

Footsteps pressed along the hallway carpet followed by a subtle, but distinct click of metal.

Deep regret swelled in Nora's chest and collided with the terror already surging through her veins. She tightened her grip on the steak knife, dark gravy dripping from its edge, and waited for the footsteps to reach her. Jeremiah had been right about not leaving the house. He was always right.

Metamorphosis
E.B. Wheeler

"Whoa!" my toddler says,
pointing her chubby finger like a wand
and infusing the world with magic.

A drooping, weather-weary tree
sheds dying leaves.
She runs through,
and they become a blazing orange trail
crackling beneath our feet.

A hedge of tattered roses,
leaf edges crisp and brown,
jealously open tissue-paper petals
and waft perfume
when she presses her nose in.

A rusted truck,
puking diesel fumes into the air,
rattles the ground.
Her wondering stare
transforms it to a mighty mechanical beast.

A cold, gray pebble,
one among many,
glints and sparkles
as prized as any diamond
when she holds it in the light.

My little girl's wide blue eyes
find magic everywhere.

The Maiden's Request
Gregory Lemon

HENRIK ADJUSTED THE silken robes sticking to his lanky frame. He hated the elaborately decorated silks he was forced to wear in the imperial palace of Chienhu. The wools and leathers of his native Rikenvatten would have been more comfortable, were it not for the oppressive heat and humidity of this foreign country. Servants walking in the hallway bowed to him as protocol required. He tried to ignore the strange looks and suppressed whispers as he passed. He thought after a couple of months the novelty of a Rikenvatten in Chienhu would have decreased. A crash down the hall caused all heads to turn. A young maid in soiled robes desperately collected the now-empty bowls and food rolling away from her silver tray. Above her, Grand Secretary Li yelled about her clumsy nature.

This was not the first time Henrik had seen the Grand Secretary lash out at servants when there were problems. The louder his shouts, the more likely it was his fault. By his overreaction, it was more likely his failing eyesight and not the maid that led to the accident.

Henrik quickly stepped into a smaller side hallway to escape. Pressed against the red wall behind one of the large golden pillars, Henrik watched the Grand Secretary shuffle past, brushing crumbs off his sleeves. Henrik avoided the Grand Secretary as much as possible.

The Grand Secretary's distrust of foreigners was well known. Henrik struggled to hide his disdain towards him.

"Hiding from the Grand Secretary again, Henrik?"

Henrik turned to find the princess sitting on a padded bench, playing with two golden meditation balls in her hand. His heart skipped a beat at her warm smile. He quickly bowed to hide the color rushing to his cheeks. "Good morning, Princess Jing."

She leaned forward and whispered, "I don't blame you. I try to avoid the old dragon whenever I can as well."

"I apologize, Princess, I meant no disrespect to the Grand Secretary."

"He enjoys finding reasons to complain where none exist. Anything new needs extra scrutiny. You and your horses are as new as they come. He prefers to be carried in his litter, no matter how slow his porters are."

She paused, and Henrik looked up. Once they locked eyes, she continued, "I'm glad that Father likes new things. I have him to thank for our meeting."

Henrik bowed again. "I'm honored by your words, Princess."

"Please, I've told you to call me Jing when my father is not around."

Henrik's heart gave another leap. "I don't know if that would be appropriate, Princess." It was Henrik's turn to lean in and whisper. She leaned forward to accept it. "The walls have ears."

Princess Jing laughed and stood. "And that's why I'm going out to the pagoda by the lake. Would you care to escort me?"

"I wish I could, Princess. I am to prepare the horses and carriage to collect Lady Nevena for tonight's banquet."

She clasped her hands with excitement. "How wonderful! Do you know why she is coming?"

"I do not. A member of the Fairy Council may request anything of any royal across the realms without explanation."

Jing pulled on her long black hair flowing down the front of her white and gold silk robes. "It is wonderful when she comes but her aura wreaks havoc on my hair."

"Your hair has always looks nice." Henrik fumbled the words while studying the patterns stitched on his shoes.

Jing smiled as she tilted her face to keep viewing Henrik's. "Have you met other fairies? Maybe some from Rikenvatten?"

The smile left Henrik's face. "Yes, I've met my share of fairies. More than I care to remember."

Princess Jing tilted her head. "I would love to hear that story, if you would like to share it."

"Maybe another time, Princess."

Henrik held the lead horse's bridle after securing the last of the equipment attaching them to the carriage. Everything was ready for its departure. He brushed the hair of the lead horse to pass the time. His mind wandered to Jing's perfect hair.

Jing was often on his mind. She alone did not treat him as foreign trash who was disrupting honored traditions with these horses. Many in Chienhu had never seen a horse before, but Jing, like her father the emperor, was excited about the benefits horses could bring to their empire. Henrik was grateful that the people of Rikenvatten had a reputation of excellent horsemanship. It made his rapid accession in the ranks of servants smooth, but there were many who resented a foreigner given so much honor and respect.

After weeks of watching the emperor and crown prince receive riding lessons from afar, Jing came close enough to ask questions about the horses. The princess confessed she thought he and the horses were oddities. Henrik was quickly smitten with her beauty. Her raven-colored hair was common in Chienhu but rarely seen in Rikenvatten.

Henrik's thoughts were shattered when Jing appeared, fleeing from the bamboo forest, clutching her hands to her chest and running as fast as her silk slippers could carry her. Their eyes met, and Henrik saw the terror within. She stopped as if to take a step toward Henrik but then continued her panicked flight to the palace.

"Oh, no," Henrik whispered. He had a feeling he knew what scared Jing but hoped he was wrong.

Henrik could not leave his position with the horses until the carriage left to collect Lady Nevena. He watched the palace closely for any sign of what had happened to Jing. After what felt like an empty eternity, the carriage left, and Henrik hurried along the path through the bamboo forest.

The path led to a small pagoda on the edge of a beautiful koi pond. The shade of the pagoda softened the heat as Henrik crossed underneath it. It had been built as a retreat from the summer sun, but the pagoda's true shelter was from the bustle of palace activity. It was easy to understand why Jing chose to spend so much time here.

Henrik approached the edge of the pond on the far side of the pagoda. A few feet away, a large flat rock barely broke through the water. He sighed as he ran his fingers through his light-yellow hair. Once he made sure he was alone, he carefully called out, "Frederik?"

A large ugly toad broke through the surface and landed on the rock. Water slowly drained off its wart-covered brown skin.

"The princess ran out of the forest terrified." Henrik sat down on a bench staring at the toad. "Would you care to share anything?"

The toad's small raspy voice scratched through the heat. "I saw an opportunity to break my curse. I was so close to getting us back home."

"That doesn't tell me what happened."

"The princess had some noisy balls and was trying to juggle them. They kept dropping and eventually one fell in. I only asked if I could retrieve it for her."

Henrik leaned forward, elbows on knees. "You actually talked to her? Oh, I'm sure that went over fantastically."

"Well, no," Frederik admitted. "She screamed."

Henrik sat up. "Of course, she screamed. She is terrified of the Cursed. Her father has filled her with horror stories about creatures like you. One word and she'd know exactly what you are."

"I'm tired of waiting in this sad insect-ridden excuse of a pond. Scaring her is better than doing nothing." Frederik stretched out his tiny legs and mumbled. "I had to try something."

"You've exposed yourself as Cursed to a member of the royal family. The emperor hates the Cursed. He'll send soldiers to hunt you down."

"I don't think she's going to tell anyone about me. If she does, she'll have to tell them about her promise."

"What promise?" Henrik slowly asked.

"I said I would get the ball for her if she promised to have me as a companion and friend in the palace, let me sit with her at the dining table, eat from her plate… "

"Are you crazy? Do you really think the princess is going to bring one of the Cursed into the palace as a dinner companion? You'd be lucky if the chef doesn't make you for dinner. What in the name of the fairies possessed you to bargain with her?"

"Since scaring her didn't work, I was hoping my request would make her angry enough."

"Obviously it didn't."

"True, but she agreed. She said the ball was precious to her, and she promised me everything I said and more. I figured that when I'm in the palace I could get her really angry and then—POOF—I'm human!"

"She was probably too scared talking with one of the Cursed to think straight," Henrik said mostly to himself.

"Well, it doesn't matter now. After I retrieved the ball, she snatched it, and ran away. I would have followed her, but I worried a crane—or worse, the palace children—would snatch me up before I got to her."

Henrik's mind spun with the complications this made in the plans to free his brother.

Frederik's croak broke the silence. "What are you going to do?"

"I don't know. I'll check on Jing and see if she's told anyone."

"Oh, is she Jing now? When did this development occur?" The toad's croak took the teasing tone Frederik's had before the Curse. Henrik was glad to hear it but was not going to respond to the inquiry.

"You stay put while I survey the damage."

"I won't go anywhere." The teasing tone was replaced by something much more bitter. "Just don't forget about me while you enjoy yourself at the palace." The toad disappeared under the water before Henrik could respond.

After he had bathed the smell of horses away and was again wearing his uncomfortable silk robes, Henrik started wandering the halls hoping to run into Jing. A nervous excitement in the servants allowed him to pass by without the normal stares. He presumed it was due to Lady Nevena's arrival. Finally, there was someone in the palace more foreign than he.

Of course, the banquet! Henrik quickened his pace until he reached the open doors to the hall. Servants lined the red walls as the royal family ate at the large circular table in the middle. Henrik slid next to one of the golden support columns for a better view. He hoped to remain hidden and wait for an opportunity to talk with Jing when she left.

Lady Nevena, the Fairy Council member who oversaw Chienhu, sat between the Emperor and Empress, the highest honor bestowed to a guest. She could have passed for a beautiful dignitary in a simple blue silk robe, were it not for the soft but visible glow from her personage. The only symbol of her Fairy Council position was the simple silver diadem encrusted with aquamarine gems that rested on her head.

The crown prince was next to his father. Jing was next to her mother, looking unsettled as she swished her utensils through her soup. Henrik wondered how much her promise to Frederik ruined her meal.

Jing looked up to find Henrik behind the servants. She tilted her head in an unasked question. Henrik had never been in the banquet hall while the royal family dined, and he guessed she was a little surprised. A small smile crossed her lips, but the concern did not leave her eyes.

Grand Secretary Li entered the hall and approached the aged emperor, failing to keep his hurried pace composed. He gently tapped the emperor's shoulder and quietly relayed a message into his ear.

The emperor whispered intensely, "A what?" The emperor's eyes darted to Jing, who avoided his gaze by sinking lower into her chair. The emperor stiffened into an angry resolve. He nodded, and the Grand Secretary motioned to a servant, who swung the door open. There on the threshold was the visitor, a large brown toad.

By this time, the whole hall had fallen silent. The only noise in the room came from the toad's approach to the circular table. The tension rose as the emperor stood.

"Stop." The emperor raised his hand. "Are you Kith or Cursed?"

"Sire, with great humility, I am one of the Cursed." A murmur spread through the hall. The toad strained to keep his voice heard. "I assure you, gracious Emperor, I am innocent and mean you neither harm nor disrespect—"

"Your assurances mean nothing. All Cursed claim to be innocent." The emperor's sharp response dripped with hatred. His response dropped to an intense whisper. "What do you want, toad?"

Henrik's muscles tensed. His brother may have caused the required royal anger, but Henrik feared his brother might not survive long enough for the curse to be broken.

"Your Majesty, I come to collect on a promise from your daughter."

All eyes of the chamber swung to Jing, who ferociously explored her wensi tofu soup.

The emperor turned his head back to the toad. "Explain."

"Earlier today, your gentle daughter was juggling her golden meditation balls at the pagoda in the bamboo forest. One ball fell into the pond, and I retrieved it for her."

"And what did she promise you?"

"She promised that I would be her constant companion."

The emperor turned to the princess. "Is that so?"

Jing's flushed face was near tears as she nodded. The face of the emperor became redder, the silk fan of the empress waved faster, and Jing tried harder to disappear in her chair. Again, Henrik expected to see his brother transform at any moment.

Nothing happened.

The emperor turned to Lady Nevena. "My Lady, I would appreciate your counsel in this matter. Is this Cursed to be trusted or executed?"

Nevena's fingers traced small, intricate patterns in the air close to her lap. Soon, the fairy stopped and smiled. "Your Majesty, the toad you see before you was once an honorable man. A moment of gallantry against those of ill intent caused him to be cursed. He can be trusted."

"Thank you, my Lady." The emperor turned his attention back to Frederik. "You shall become my daughter's companion." Jing let out an involuntary squeal in protest. The emperor tensed as he continued,

"You may enter the palace, but you are not, under any circumstances, to enter her chambers."

"Thank you, Your Highness." The toad shifted toward the fairy. "Thank you, my Lady. Your benevolence is greatly appreciated."

Lady Nevena nodded.

The emperor swept his hand from Jing to the toad. "Well?"

"Father, no!"

"He helped you in your time of need. You are duty bound to do as you promised."

"But, Father!"

He raised his hand to silence her.

Jing's eyes swept across the hall, desperately searching for help. "Father, may I request a servant to help care for my new companion?"

The emperor thought for a moment. "You may. Who?"

"Henrik, the horse master."

The old lotus seat cushion Henrik carried down the palace hallway provided little padding. It was difficult to see the warty toad resting on its dusty brown surface. No one could have found a more insulting vessel to carry the newest royal companion, and Henrik was sure the emperor tried.

The princess and her attendant slowly walked in front of Henrik. Jing stopped at a bench and sat. "Please go and prepare my chambers for the night and wait for me there."

The attendant bowed and left them alone. Jing put her face in her hands and let out a groan of frustration. "Henrik, what am I supposed to do?"

"Princess, I—"

Her face shot up out of her hands, and she yelled, "I forbid you from calling me Princess ever again!" The flash of anger was gone as quickly as it came, replaced by a resigned sadness. It hung between them like a heavy curtain. After a moment, she gently patted the open space next to her. "Please sit with me."

Henrik sat, subtly turning the cushion and the toad away from her view. No matter how he turned the cushion, the toad shifted to look at the princess.

"My father is furious with the shame I've brought to the palace. That"—pointing at the toad—"is the first Cursed to enter the palace since my father banished the previous Grand Secretary for treachery. He loved him as a son and trusted him like a brother. When the betrayal was discovered, Lady Nevena cursed him to be a golden tree snake, fast enough to flee, but too weak to harm humans." Jing leaned her head back against the wall. "I was young at the time, but I still remember my father's hurt and anger. I never wanted to be the cause of something like that. And that is what I have done tonight."

Her eyes filled with tears as they sat together in extended silence. She reached out and gently took Henrik's hand. She smiled as they looked at each other. "Thanks for listening."

The toad said, "Is there anything I can do to help?"

"You want to help?" Jing leaped from the bench as her tears returned. "Leave! Leave this palace and never look at me again!"

Henrik and his brother barely spoke after entering the servants' buildings. He placed the cushion on the floor of his room and went straight to bed without changing. Visions of Jing running and crying haunted Henrik's attempt to sleep. The desire to fix the harm Frederik's actions had caused kept him awake. Guilt mixed into his thoughts because he thought more of Jing than his cursed brother.

Henrik rolled over to check on the toad. The cushion was empty. He shot out of bed and walked quickly toward the palace, searching, and hoping he wouldn't attract a patrolling guard's attention. Henrik neared Jing's chambers when a woman's scream startled him.

"Jing!" Henrik rushed to open the door to the chamber. In the dim light from torches outside the window, he only saw the closed drapes of Jing's canopy bed.

"You foul creature!"

The toad came flying out from behind the drapes. Henrik ducked and heard a loud thud on the wall behind him, followed by a much larger crash on the floor.

The attendant rushed to the bed and opened the silken bed curtains. She sat and spoke calming words at the princess's side. "My lady, are you all right? What happened?" Fury coursed through Jing's eyes as she pointed to where she had thrown the toad.

Henrik heard shouts from soldiers running along the halls. He turned to see a broad-shouldered man groaning and stirring in the corner. The man's arms and legs fumbled as if he had forgotten how to use them. Henrik grabbed a discarded robe and covered him. "Frederik, you idiot!" Henrik pulled Frederik to his feet. "We need to get out of here, now!"

Jing screamed again. "Frederik? Who's Frederik?"

"Jing, this is my older brother."

The anger on her face shifted to a confused panic as her glare shifted between both men. She whispered to Henrik. "You can't be found here!"

"I did it, Henrik. I broke the curse. We can go home!"

Soldiers burst through the chamber doors. The two men did not resist as they were forced to the ground and tied with ropes.

Henrik and Frederik stood in the middle of the royal court, waiting for the emperor. They were surrounded by palace guards, and their ropes replaced with iron shackles and chains.

"You look pretty good, all things considering," Henrik said. "But I still think you are an idiot."

Frederik chuckled as he rolled his shoulders but then winced. "It hurt more to transform this time."

"That was probably the impact with the wall."

Frederik looked down. "Couldn't you have grabbed a man's robe?"

Indistinct yelling could be heard from the hall outside the room. The doors behind them slammed open, and the emperor stormed to the throne. "Are these the foul scum?" he bellowed.

The empress and Jing entered the hall and came alongside the wall. Jing's eyes were red. She looked like she had run out of tears. The empress gently held her shoulders as they stayed in the far corner.

The emperor paced back and forth in a rage. He sized up Frederik and had a new look of hatred for Henrik. Finally, he broke his furious silence. "How dare you enter into my daughter's chambers! You will both be executed for your crimes against the crown."

Lady Nevena entered the hall. Her blue robes glowed brighter in the hall as the servants were still rushing to light candles around the room. "Dear Emperor, I believe you should hear them before you continue." Her demeanor was calm, but there was radiant authority behind her statement. It was not a request.

"Hear them? They will be executed! Traitorous thieves who were caught with my daughter!"

"I snuck into the palace," said Frederik. "He tried to stop me."

Henrik shushed him.

The emperor's face leaped between the brothers, his family, and the fairy. After a moment of swirling glances, he let out a quick huff and turned to sit on his throne. He motioned for all to take chairs along the wall. The empress and princess took their places in the smaller thrones at his side.

"I will hear you, as requested by Lady Nevena."

Frederik stepped forward, and the guards drew their swords to keep him in his place.

"Most honorable Emperor, my name is Frederik. I am the son of King Ulrik and Queen Caroline, Crown Prince of Rikenvatten." He swung his shackled hands to his right. "This is Prince Henrik of Rikenvatten, my younger brother."

The shock of this proclamation spread to all who were in the room. Lady Nevena smiled and said, "Emperor, these men speak the truth and are men of honor, as I stated before."

"Honorable men are not caught in my daughter's chambers!" yelled the emperor. A stern look from Lady Nevena and an increase in the glow of her aura forced him to compose himself. "Explain," he growled at Prince Frederik.

"Your Excellency and court of Chienhu, last year my brother and I were traveling through our kingdom and came upon a gang of thieves stealing from a royal outpost. As I led the charge against them, I was transformed into a toad by an evil fae in their number. My brother returned us home, seeking a means to restore me to human form. Those who wished to usurp our family's reign claimed that Henrik murdered me and concocted a fantastical tale to claim the throne for himself. We both had to flee the country until I could be restored. My faithful brother knew I could not survive a winter near our native land, so he brought me here, cared for me, and secured service with Your Majesty."

"That does not explain why you committed this treachery against my daughter."

Lady Naveen interrupted. "Breaking a curse, such as this one your Majesty, varies depending on who casts the spell. It appears the fae intended to sow additional harm to Rikenvatten by requiring an outburst of royal anger to break this curse."

Frederik nodded and continued. "We meant no harm to Your Highness, your family, or your empire. We believed many times that the curse was about to be broken. I alone entered your daughter's chamber in a desperate attempt to anger her. My brother was too late to stop me." Frederik bowed before the Emperor. "I humbly beg your forgiveness, Your Majesty. We only request that you allow us passage that we may return to our family in Rikenvatten and clear my brother of the false murder charges."

Jing whimpered. Her eyes met with Henrik's, and they shared a long gaze.

The emperor pointed to the princess. "You think I could so easily forgive you when my daughter is in such a state?"

"No, Father," Jing said. "That is not what I meant. Please do not harm them." She pointed at Henrik. "I … I love him."

The emperor stared at his daughter. "He tends the horses. How could you fall in love with a servant?"

"He's a prince from a foreign land," Jing said.

The emperor's eyes narrowed at his daughter. "Did you know?"

"No," Jing looked at Henrik. "He never told me who he was, but there always was something more about him that I could not ignore."

Henrik stepped forward. "If it pleases Your Majesty, may I speak?"

The emperor slumped back. "This is madness." He waved his hand granting permission.

"We are truly sorry for the harm and distress that we have caused. I hid this from Your Majesty and Highnesses so that those who sought our demise would not hear rumors of our location and put your subjects in danger if they followed us here. Our kingdom is in peril from those who would destroy our family. It is imperative that we leave and restore my brother's claim to the throne."

Henrik turned to Jing. "I am sorry that I could never tell you who I was. Your kindness sustained me through this trial. If my kingdom were not in peril, I would ask your father for your hand." Henrik stared deeply into the eyes he had long cherished. "I love you, Jing."

Jing clasped her hands to her mouth and laughed through new tears. She cautiously looked at both of her parents and then leaped from her throne. Henrik almost lost his footing as she threw her arms around his neck. "I will come with you."

"You will do no such thing!" bellowed the emperor.

The empress reached out and placed her hand on the emperor's. With the faintest touch, his protest was silenced.

Henrik, still in chains, moved so that he could look into Jing's eyes. "Your father is right. You must stay here."

"I don't care," she whispered.

"I care."

"Will you ever return?"

"Henrik the horse master needs to leave. But I will return as Prince Henrik of Rikenvatten and court you properly."

"I don't care what you're called. Just promise you'll come back to me."

"I promise."

Hunger Moon
Sariah Horowitz

BOTH FRONT TIRES sat jammed, in front and behind, against at least six inches of ice. Keith had been mentally cursing for the last hour as they'd tried to push the truck out of the ice-covered hole in the middle of the dirt road. He and three other students were heading back to campus after exploring the desert mountains of Southern Utah. Now, their truck was sunk up to the hubs in a large frozen puddle in the late afternoon. They'd used the all-wheel-drive, put it in reverse, used the truck mats, even bruised their hands trying to break off branches from the stubborn sagebrush surrounding them.

It was supposed to be just a ride through the mountains. Now, Keith regretted suggesting they follow the GPS coordinates through the back roads. Several hours of fun adventuring were wiped away by getting stuck. It was February and the sun was already hanging low in the distance.

Sweaty and tired, everyone stopped trying to lift. They climbed out of the puddle. The weight of the truck seemed to be driving the girls farther into the mud. Their shoes and pant legs were soaked. Especially Ronda, the smallest of the group; the water went to her knees. Sweat glistened on their faces as they leaned heavily against the truck. Lydia's long hair was falling all over her face, escaping from her braids. Morris readjusted the glasses sliding down his nose.

"Want to try the truck again?" Morris asked.

Keith looked down at the ice. "It's not working."

"I thought we could lift it out." Morris frowned.

"It's a double cab pickup truck, Muscles. Not a smart car," Keith snarled.

"I thought the sagebrush did some traction." Lydia's voice was sarcastic.

All of them looked around the desolate landscape for options. They had the worst collection of people to lift a truck out of the ice. Lydia played volleyball but didn't have amazing weight lifting skills. Morris studied English and ran pizza delivery. Keith was tall and in good shape, but he was no bodybuilder. He was, in fact, a computer nerd who now wished he was back at his dorm finishing his English paper on "Queueing Theory." The fourth member of the group, Ronda, was a small, black-haired girl from Lydia's dorm whom Keith barely knew. Quite the group to be stuck with.

It felt as if it had only been a few hours since they'd been standing in the lobby of the dorm looking for adventure. Apparently, they'd found that. The sun shone brightly that morning, making the 30 degrees at the 6100-foot elevation seem warmer than it was. It had been fun skidding down the backroads and hills. Not another vehicle had appeared in the desolate winter mountains of Southern Utah with no red rocks to attract tourists. It had seemed like a good idea at first. They thought about driving to Bryce Canyon or Zion National Park but opted to drive around the ice-covered dirt roads. No worries. Morris' truck had four-wheel drive. Smart, Keith chided himself.

North of Cedar City was higher elevation. Now, they were over 8000 feet surrounded by a blanket of snow speckled in sagebrush. Hills rose on either side in waves dividing them from the outside world. Keith could see the peaks of higher mountains like islands on the horizon.

"It looks like we're stuck here for the night."

"No, we can't." Ronda's arms were wrapped around her middle in an attempt to stay warm.

"Should we walk out?" Morris said.

"Walk where?" Lydia said, "There's nothing around here."

"The highway can't be too far away: only around five miles or so."

Ronda looked up at the suggestion.

"We can't do that." Keith motioned at the horizon. "It's getting late."

"Then we better get started," Morris said.

"And freeze to death," Keith said. "Don't you read the newspaper? Last year some students tried walking out of these mountains when they got stuck up here around Halloween."

"They didn't make it?" Lynda guessed.

"Found their bodies in the spring after everything thawed," Keith said.

"That doesn't mean it will happen to us." Ronda's voice seemed on the brink of cracking. "We can't stay the night."

Keith and his friends shared glances. The situation was stressful enough, but this girl seemed particularly freaked out about staying out all night.

"Are we positive the phones aren't working?" Lydia asked for the millionth time.

Only Morris pulled out his phone. None of the other phones had any signal, and only Morris' phone would flick in and out of bars.

Morris walked around trying to get reception.

"Damn, it's almost dead," Morris muttered. "Stupid bars won't stay long enough to send something off."

"Use the truck," Ronda suggested. "It's metal. Maybe it will help."

Morris climbed into the bed of the truck. He stood waving his phone over his head.

"Yes, got a message off." His phone beeped. "And there goes the battery."

"Great." Keith attempted to scrape mud off one shoe with the other. All it accomplished was spreading the mud around.

"What did you send off?" Ronda asked.

"SOS and our GPS location." Morris jumped out of the bed and into the snow with a crunch. "Maybe Justin will come get us."

"Justin? Your roommate?"

"He's my first contact." Morris sounded defensive.

"Good luck with that." Lydia scoffed. "Unless you've got the right body parts, he doesn't read your messages."

"I was being optimistic," Morris said.

Lydia walked over to him and rested her head on his shoulder. "It was a smart thought. At least someone has information of where we are."

The two of them started hugging and being mushy. Keith turned away. Maybe walking out would be better than staying in the same truck with those two.

A movement made him look towards the truck. Ronda stood in the puddle, trying to lift the truck. She looked almost crazed as she tugged. The smallest of the four pulling against the truck showed how futile their efforts had been.

"Hey, Ronda, take it easy," Keith said.

"We have to get out of here." She almost slipped but still held the metal body of the truck. The mud puddle seemed to be sucking it in like chocolate quicksand.

Keith put his hands under Ronda's armpits and lifted her up. She hung onto the truck, the middle of a tug of war.

"Let go," Keith said.

"Girl, you're crazy," Lydia said.

Size difference finally prevailed, and Keith pulled her away. He walked several feet away from the truck and set her down in the snow. She looked at the ground, avoiding eye contact. Red lines on her hands seemed only moments from splitting open.

"What were you thinking?" Keith demanded.

Ronda looked up at him as if she going to say something, then she shoved her hands in her coat pockets and looked back at the ground.

"I need to get home," she said.

Keith looked around, but no one offered any help.

"Hey, it's going to work out. Just calm down."

He walked back to the truck. The others gave him a look but he only shrugged. He didn't know what to say. They weren't going to get out for several hours and panicking wouldn't help.

"We better get in the truck," Morris said.

They piled into the back seat of the double cab.

"Turn on the heater."

"No, it's only at a fourth of a tank. I'll need it to drive out of here in the morning."

"We're not going to be driving anywhere if we freeze" Lydia pointed out.

"We'll need to stay close together."

"Tell her that." Lydia pointed out the window. Ronda was still standing out in the cold.

"We can't let her stay out there," Keith said.

"Why not? She doesn't want to be with us." Morris shrugged.

"And what are we going to tell the cops if they come across her frozen body and us alive in the cab."

"You don't have to be morbid," Morris said.

"I'll talk to her." Lydia slipped out of the truck.

"Why did she come anyway?" Keith asked.

Morris breathed on his hands, trying to warm them. "She lives on Lydia's floor. I assumed they were friends."

"You and Lydia have been friends since last semester. You don't know anything about her?"

"Dude, she's not her roommate. Besides, she's only been on campus this semester. Not a lot of time to get to know someone."

"True." It was only Presidents' Day weekend. A month into the semester didn't give much time to know a recluse like Ronda.

Keith rolled down his window to tell the girls to hurry it up, then realized he could hear what they were saying. The two girls stood only a few feet away from the truck.

"No, we have to go." Ronda shook, probably from the cold.

"Nothing is going to happen," Lydia said. "It's not like you're tempting at all. It's just for tonight. We'll be able to walk out in the morning. Do you have a problem with surviving?"

Ronda bit her nails, glancing around the barren wilderness. Finally, she nodded and followed Lydia into the truck. She sat down next to Keith and avoided eye contact. She picked up her water bottle and took a long drink.

"Hey, save your water," Keith said. "The snow probably isn't fresh."

She finally put the bottle down with a few inches of liquid left.

"Is there any food?" Ronda asked.

"Umm," Morris said. "Does anyone have anything?"

Everyone searched their pockets. The only edible product was a fun size Twix in Lydia's jacket. She looked at the finger length candy with disappointment.

"We all have water, but we're going to have to split this four ways," she said.

"I guess we could do cannibalism" Keith suggested.

Morris and Lydia laughed.

"I'm the oldest," Lydia said dramatically. "I've lived long enough."

Ronda made a snorting sound that probably was supposed to be a laugh. She blushed at their stares and began chewing off some purple nail polish.

The sun bobbed above the horizon before finally melting. The temperature plummeted. Shadows spread like sinister cloaks of unknown inhabitants in the orange-red glow of dusk.

"We need to stay close together to stay warm."

"I call Morris." Lydia scooted next to her friend.

Keith and Ronda glanced at each other. Keith's face felt warmer than the rest of him. Ronda pulled the cuffs of her jacket over her hands and hunched over, arms across her stomach in a protective position. Keith could take a hint. The side of the truck was cold but it was as much space as he could give her.

The landscape stretched away on all sides around them in an endless blanket of snow and sagebrush. Hills rippled to the horizon where the distant mountain tops stood like giant sentries keeping the outside world out of reach. The marooned feeling became more impressed in Keith's mind.

Somewhere beyond the snow-covered hills were the highway, city buildings, and university campus. The guys would be doing their nightly Halo tournament in Ted's room, eating a never-ending supply of snacks. The old faded carpet and drafty halls of Juniper Hall seemed like the Ritz right now.

Lydia and Morris were taking the 'keeping each other warm' to the next level. The two of them became a tangle of limbs and giggles.

Keith looked at his watch. It was after five. The other students would be heading to the cafeteria. He would welcome the dry meat and damp pizza at this moment. His stomach growled.

"Are you cold?" Ronda asked.

"A little, but I'm good." It was a lie, but he didn't want her to feel obligated. "You?"

"I'm fine."

She was shaking. He remembered her saying once that she had a condition that caused her problems when she didn't have regular meals.

"You can have the candy if you want."

She shook her head. "No thanks." He kept looking out the windshield as if waiting for something, maybe help, to appear over the horizon.

Darkness thickened outside the truck. The overhead light in the cab soon became the only light source. Lydia and Morris seemed to become bored with cuddling and were attempting to fit in the same jacket.

Keith heard a loud click next to him. Looking down, he realized Ronda had fastened the center seat belt across her middle and was tightening it.

"What are you doing?" Lynda had also noticed.

"You need to move," Ronda said

"What?"

She pressed herself more and more against the back of the seat. "All of you need to move."

"Are you out of your mind?" Lydia said.

"This is my truck," Morris cut in.

"I'm going to be sick." Her voice shook and she looked paler than usual.

The others shared looks. No one wanted vomit on them.

The three scrambled into the front seat after several moments of a foot to the face and three people trying to climb onto the bench seat at the same time.

"Shouldn't we try to keep her warm?" Keith suggested.

They looked back at Ronda. She was squished into the back of the seat as far away from them as possible curled up in a fetal position with the seatbelt strained around her middle.

"I don't think she wants it," Lydia said.

The front of the cab felt colder. The front doors must have been letting in a draft. The three of them huddled together with Lydia sandwiched between them.

"I shouldn't have asked her to come," Lydia muttered. "She always makes things awkward. That's what I get for being nice."

Keith silently agreed. Ronda wasn't really their friend. She was a girl from the dorm who hung around them. She seemed to like them but was always skulking by the walls or sitting in the corner watching. Now she was the one getting sick. How were they all going to walk out in the morning? How were they going to get through the night?

Darkness took over the world outside. This far away from Cedar City, there wasn't a glow from the city lights. The clear sky sucked all warmth away. Teeth chattered as the three huddled together in an attempt to keep warm. Minutes ticked on. No one even looked up when someone's stomach growled.

"Can we please turn on the truck to get some heat?" Lydia's teeth chattered.

"We need to save gas," Morris said.

"Just for a few minutes."

"Alright."

"Wait!" Keith motioned out the windshield. On the black horizon, a yellow glow began to rise.

"Is it headlights?" Morris said.

The three watched anxiously.

The moon's round face appeared from behind the mountain peaks.

Lydia's middle finger stood out against the moon. Keith muttered an obscenity.

Moonlight flowed inside the cab, reflected on the back of the faded upholstery.

Whimpering came from the back of the cab. The truck began to shake as if something was trying to escape.

"Oh please," Lydia snapped. "We're all hungry, girl. Get a grip."

The whimpers and shaking stopped.

A thud came from the back of the cab. Keith looked in the back. The fasten seatbelt sat alone on the bench seat. The ceiling light cast dark shadows along the floor of the truck. Keith opened his mouth to tell the others, but the words died in his throat.

Something slid from the shadow of the cab floor. Yellow-orange fur glowed in the light as a human-size coyote climbed onto the back seat. Yellow eyes turned on Keith. The creature shook itself like a dog. Morris and Lydia turned around at the sound.

"What the—?" Morris was cut off by Lydia's scream.

A rumble came from the coyote. It was too short for a growl. Keith knew it from hearing for the last hour. It was the stomach growl. The creature was hungry.

A real growl rumbled through the cab. Keith's back hit the steering wheel. The horn blared in his ears, but he kept pressing. Lydia and Morris pressed themselves against the glove compartment.

Hand-sized paws hooked around the seat, flaking nail polish like blood on white claws. The gap between the three and the back seat seemed to shrink. The creature leaned in close, hackles raised.

Its tongue ran along its white fangs.

Keith's hand found the door handle. Falling through the door, he hit the snow with a shock of cold. Lydia screamed. Keith didn't dare look back. Crawling through the chunks of ice, he made his way through the snow. Sagebrush and ice tore at him, but he didn't stop.

The snow glowed in the moonlight. Shadows seemed to spin. Teeth chattering, Keith looked back the way he came. The cab light shone in the distance. He couldn't go back. He had to get help.

He kept crawling. His face and hands were numb with cold, his pant legs and shoes soaked from the icy water now frozen stiff as he tried to make his way farther down the road. His lungs burned with each breath. He became so tired, so very tired. He wanted to sleep. No, he must keep going. Keith slipped, his head hitting the snow. Just a short rest. Eyelids grew heavy. His shivers slowed.

Yellow circles shone in the distance.

A Body of Work
Denis Feehan

My father once gave me
A piece of his mind
Keep your nose to the grindstone
And the gods will be kind.

I turned a deaf ear to
His lecture and said
I would stick my fool neck out
I would make my own bed.

He said you got nerve but
No stomach for work.
I replied have a heart, Dad,
You were once a young Turk

With skin in the game and
Your eyes on the prize
And you shouldered the burden
Much to Grandpa's surprise.

Dad laughed when I told him
I'd knuckle on down
That I'd soon get a leg up
On the clowns in our town.

See, Dad said it comes down
To elbow grease, son,
About showing some backbone
Not just havin' fun.

I knew that my dad had
A nose for the truth
So I took up employment
with my first cousin Ruth.

So now I'm a banker
And earning a check,
But I got to be honest
It's a pain in the neck.

Except for my Mustang
And cool bachelor pad
I guess working my fingers
To the bone ain't so bad.

Thanks, Dad.

Marie
David Rodeback

I met Marie in the hallway after school. "The race is tomorrow," I said. "We should sign up."

"The three-legged race?"

"Yeah."

Running the three-legged race together was what seventh-grade couples did on the next-to-last day of school, at the Outdoor Games.

For two months Marie and I had sat together at lunch, in assemblies, and on field trips. Being a couple was way better than her poking me in the back with her pencil in Algebra. I'd never been so happy. I had already prepared something to write in her yearbook on the last day of school—right after the morning movie, where I hoped to hold her hand for the first time.

"I'm sorry, Kenny." Her big, brown eyes matched her words.

"You don't want to race?"

"No, I do."

"I don't understand."

I thought I saw her chin quiver, and she looked down. "I already signed up."

"Oh, good. I didn't know. Think we'll win?"

I liked her blond curls, her sprinkling of freckles, and her smile. But she wasn't smiling now.

"Not with you. With Bobby."

Maybe my heart didn't stop, but it started to hurt—for two reasons. The second one was, Bobby was my best friend.

"With … Bobby?"

She seemed relieved. "I'm sorry. I didn't know how to tell you."

Later, I was glad that what I said next wasn't angry or mean.

"Well, you told me." I started to turn away, then turned back. "Um, good luck. You know. In the race. With, um … you know."

Then I did turn away. She said she was sorry again. I nodded without looking back.

I walked home in a daze, told Mom I was sick and wouldn't want dinner, collapsed on my bed, tried not to cry, and thought about how much it hurt.

I must have fallen asleep eventually, and Mom or Dad must have pulled a thin blanket over me. It was dark when I awoke, and the house was quiet. I couldn't get back to sleep.

Instead, I had daydreams. I figured they were still daydreams, even at night, because I was awake.

In my first daydream, I cheered for Bobby and Marie, and they won. After they untied their legs, Marie ran to hug me, not Bobby, and we walked away, holding hands.

In my second daydream, Bobby hugged April, the girl he had liked before. Marie kissed my cheek in front of everybody.

In my third daydream, she hugged me, then pulled me away, and we went and sat under a tree. She apologized (tearfully) and said Bobby was nice (which I knew), but I was the boy she really liked. Then she kissed me on both cheeks. I dried her tears with the clean handkerchief Mom made me keep in my pocket, which I hadn't pulled out at school since kindergarten, because it was embarrassing, except when I used it to dry a girl's tears.

What actually happened was, in the morning I told Mom I was still sick. I didn't want to eat, so she believed me. I watched World War II documentaries on the History Channel all day.

On the last half-day of school, I sat at the front of the cafeteria for the movie, *Camelot*, so I couldn't see Marie sitting with Bobby.

Afterward, I picked up my yearbook, flipped through it, and decided not to stay for the signing. On my way to the front doors I ran into Marie. She was alone. Her eyes were big, and her voice was soft.

"Hi, Kenny."

"Hi."

"Did you like the movie?"

I shrugged. "The first part was fun."

"The last part was too sad," she said.

"Did you win the race?" I asked.

"No, but it was fun. Are you okay? They said you were sick."

"A little better today."

"That's good."

We both saw Bobby approaching. "So, uh, see you later," she said. "Have a nice summer."

"You too."

As soon as I was outside, I broke into a run.

At home I dropped my yearbook on the kitchen table—I wanted to throw it at the wall—and sat on my bed, updating my daydreams so that Marie visited me at home, since school was out for the summer.

I must have fallen asleep again. I awoke when Mom knocked and opened my door.

"Still sick, honey?"

"Yeah."

"I'm sorry. You came home before anyone signed your yearbook?"

"Yeah."

"A girl came by while you were asleep. Mary? Marie? She wanted to sign it, and she seemed nice, so I let her. She left hers for you to sign. She'll pick it up later."

"She signed my yearbook?"

"Yes. Shall I get it?"

"Yeah. Thanks."

She brought both yearbooks and a pen, then stood in the doorway, watching me.

"Thanks, Mom. I'll sign it later."

"Okay."

"Did you read what she wrote?" I asked.

"Not without permission. It's not my yearbook."

"Okay."

She finally left.

I sat up and tried to invent a daydream about Marie being my eighth-grade girlfriend. I couldn't make it work. Finally, I reached for my yearbook and opened the front cover.

There it was.

"Dear Kenny,

"We had a fun year. You're nice. Sorry I made you sad. Please don't hate Bobby. Sometimes things just happen.

"I need to thank you for something. When you saw me today, you didn't pretend I wasn't there, and you weren't angry or mean. You talked to me, and when I said have a nice summer, you said, you too.

"You're a good guy. You deserve a great summer.

"Your friend, Marie."

A week earlier, she would have dotted the i's in "friend" and "Marie" with little hearts. Now they were just dots.

I opened her yearbook, didn't look for what Bobby had written, found my picture, and wrote in the margin next to it, "Marie, it was a fun year. Have a happy summer. Kenny"

I closed the book.

It was over.

My daydreams were stupid.

And it hurt.

Red River Church
Marie Tollstrup

ADDICTED TO INNER-TUBING the serene river's flow, we older sisters attend Red River church. Wildflowers incense the breeze as we fly and float, float and fly. The river's hallowed current cleanses household eruptions. The stream's hymnal song flows reverently as nuns worship in chapel and wings our prayers heavenward. The wind swishes columned trees, sacred walls hugging the dappled river's edge, and purifies our taut bones.

Gurgling water announce barbed-boulders in our path, a passing dissonance to our spiritual elevation. Blue heron's wingspread sweeps above the river's aisle. We marvel at its winged grace and wave to a fellow parishioner. Profound tranquility settles into our marrow, a blessing, as our communion with water regains life's symmetry. When insomnia strikes, I attend Red River church to fly and float, float and fly, inner-tubing its serene drift.

The Piglet
Felicia Rose

SOMETIME IN THE SPRING of 1978 our seventh-grade class ventured beyond the confines of the dilapidated Brooklyn synagogue that doubled as our school, and spent the day in a hamlet upstate New York. Two photographs mark that day. In the first, twenty-three somber-looking girls, all wearing long navy skirts and long-sleeved shirts, stand in two rows facing the camera. Behind us is a blurry daisy-filled pasture. In the second, Batya, my best friend at the time, stands unsmiling beside a water wheel, her long flaxen braids ending at still narrow hips. The photographs stir little memory of that day, and I remember little of it, except this.

After a tour of old log cabins, the teachers, two stern women in their thirties, both wearing ritual wigs, allowed us to roam through the gift shop. Batya and I tarried in a quiet corner looking at ceramic figurines. One of the Madonna and Child caught our eye; immediately, we shifted our gaze. A mere glance might corrupt our souls, taint our resolute faith.

Our Orthodox Jewish girls' school inculcated us with that faith in nearly every lesson we learned. Pray every morning and night; pray before and after meals; pray when kissing the *mezuzah* (a small oblong black box containing a parchment with verses from Deuteronomy), which hangs from the doorjambs of observant Jewish homes. Never wear pants; those are for boys. Always cover elbows, collarbones, knees. When you marry, cover your hair. Obey your parents. The Fifth Commandment demands it. Thank God for making you according to His will. (The males of the tribe thanked God for not making them female.) Never eat dairy within six hours of eating meat. Never eat shellfish or pork.

Like nearly all the girls in our *yeshiva*, Batya lived these laws at school and at home. I, whose mother had rebelled against the orthodoxy of her parents, lived them mainly at school. (Should I obey my mother when she told me to eat the ham on my plate? Afraid to ask my teachers, I never resolved it.)

At school, desperately wanting to belong, I compensated for this unmentionable sin of familial sacrilege by committing myself to piety. Morning *davening* consisted of thirty minutes of group prayer followed by silent devotions. Many of the girls, undoubtedly bored by the mindless repetition of gesture and word, recited the group orison with the speed of a professional auctioneer, and then claimed, by virtue of taking their seats, to have completed the silent supplication.

Not I. Each morning, prayer book in hand, I swayed fervently to and fro, bowed deeply, beat my chest at the proper times. Having memorized most of these Hebrew prayers, I sometimes closed my eyes. Occasionally, I cried.

Fridays we had half days of school so we could be home in time to help our mothers prepare for the Sabbath, which begins at sunset. Many a Friday I went home with Batya and stayed for the weekend. (I lived at a distance from her home, and since the use of vehicles is forbidden on *Shabbos*, I waited until Sunday so I could take the bus or else stayed until Monday and travelled to school with her.) Despite the presence of her five, then six, then seven younger siblings, the house exuded calm. In that ambience, we helped her mother roast chicken, bake *challah* bread, prepare soup. Since the meal would involve meat, we took care to use the utensils, dishes and counters reserved for *fleishig* food. Before dinner, we lit the Sabbath candles with Batya's mother and said the appropriate prayer. We performed the ritual hand washing – *n'tilat yadayim* – three streams of water over the right hand followed by three over the left. Silence. Then we prayed, and took a bite of the *challah* we had braided and baked. We listened to Batya's father say the prayer for wine. We replied, "Amen." After dinner, we prayed the protracted *birkat hamazon* to thank God for a meal that included grain. Before sleep, we put our right hand over our eyes and prayed *shema*.

In the ten years we remained friends, Batya visited my home but twice. Both times it was a Sunday. Both times I knew in advance Mother would be away. In preparation for Batya's arrival, I rearranged the refrigerator so that *milchig* foods – milk, yogurt, butter – occupied the top shelf while *fleishig* victuals – a piece of meatloaf, a leg of chicken – took their place on the bottom. *Pareve* food, mostly in the form of vegetables and fruit, occupied the drawers. I buried the cans of non-kosher meat in the back of the cabinet, displayed boxes of matzo meal, high priests of the kosher-food kingdom, up front.

I laid a towel on the right side of the sink for the dairy utensils. The dish drain on the left would be for those used for meat. Several dishes of one pattern sat on one side; some of a different pattern rested on the other. The appearance of a kosher kitchen prevailed.

Thanks to grandfather, a *mezuzah* hung on the frame of our apartment door. Mother had allowed me to hang a second one on the doorframe of my bedroom. Now, I used double-faced tape to adhere additional ones to the entry of the remaining rooms of our apartment.

I carefully orchestrated the lunch preparations. The tuna can with the kosher certification sat on the counter. Ditto the rye bread and mayo. When Batya arrived, we made tuna sandwiches together. "Would you mind handing me the can opener?" I asked. "Let's use the *milchig* one so we can drink milk with our meal."

What did I hope to accomplish from this charade? To prove to Batya I lived a devout life? To preclude the shame of difference? To demonstrate that I belonged?

Did Batya believe it? Probably not. Despite my efforts, countless subtle – and not so subtle – distinctions remained. Why didn't I invite her to spend the Sabbath? Why did my mother, whom Batya had seen at school events, not cover her hair with a scarf or ritual wig? Why had my parents divorced?

In the end, I imagine Batya didn't care. If anything, my non-religious home life may have intrigued her. (More than once, she asked to try on a pair of my pants, which she knew I owned.) Or else she enjoyed our friendship, and that was what mattered.

Shortly after shunning the Madonna and Child, we came upon a collection of animal figurines.

"Oh, the chicken's so cute," Batya said.

"Do you think that's the souvenir you'll buy?

"Oh, I don't know. The duck's cute, too. My sister Sarah would adore it." For several minutes we examined the display, once or twice lifting a ceramic animal to study more closely.

"Upright in every way," teachers wrote on my report card. "Like her namesake, Fruma is pious and devout. A young woman who abides by Jewish law."

Preoccupied with belonging in a way those who came from Orthodox families did not, I had never before rebelled. Yet at that moment, an unknown impulse gripped me, and I lifted the piglet. Yes, I touched a ceramic rendition of a baby pig.

Batya gasped. "My father would never allow me to do that." I imagined her father, a rotund man with a long black beard and side curls. Always, he wore a black suit and white shirt, prompting Batya to say, "When I see a bunch of men walking to synagogue together, I can't tell from behind which is my father." What would this staunch, distant man do if he knew Batya had touched the very symbol of *treyf*: dirty, non-kosher, no less blasphemous than the Madonna and Child?

"He'd probably make me wash really well, and then pray to *Hashem* for forgiveness," she said, as if guessing my thoughts. "I wouldn't be allowed to play outside for a week."

Why had I done it? I knew pork was forbidden, that the slightest regard for anything porcine constituted blasphemy.

I can only guess what the motives of my twelve-year-old self had been. A rare moment of risk-taking in an otherwise timid child? A desire for authenticity? Hope that Batya would join me beyond the confines of her rigid world?

"I should wash my hands," I said.

Batya surveyed the gift shop for a restroom. Pointing to one, she reached back with her other hand, and while not quite looking as Lot's wife had done, but not entirely without looking either, she patted the piglet.

"Let's go," she said.

I removed from my book bag a small bar of kosher soap. In a prayer of contrition, we washed our hands.

Klatch
Tim Keller

SAILOR DIDN'T LIKE the looks of the young man; that much was clear. "Whoo-boy," he said, "would you look who's here. Talk about a bad penny turning up."

The young man—not much more than a boy really—burrowed into the meager shade of the drinking fountain in front of my father's service station, folded his arms over a leather vest and, in spite of the scorching heat of a cloudless July day, fell asleep.

"Just look at how he's dressed!" Sailor continued. "Hair all flapping around like a girl's— damn hippie! Probably squats to pee."

My face reddened, but a look from Dad silenced even the hint of protest. Didn't they know who that was? They'd cheered for him often enough from the stands. Richie Buttars was the guy every boy wanted to be and every girl wanted to have. He had the skills: legendary on the basketball court. He had the car: a black '79 Camaro Z28, complete with orange racing stripe. And he had the style: that awesome leather vest and never even a hair out of place. But school'd been out for six whole weeks now, a lifetime ago apparently.

Sailor, for his part, was dressed to the nines in shabby coveralls and worn work boots, looking every bit the male part in *American Gothic*, the stifling of which observation, again at the psychic behest of my father, actually hurt.

"Kid came sniffin' around my daughter, I'd fill his rear end so full of rock salt, it'd shrivel up like a couple of raisins."

"What daughter?" I said under my breath amidst the laughter. Not quietly enough; Dad's finger rapped my skull.

"I hear old Harris ran him outta Premium Oil," Ike Condie said. "Wouldn't even let him fill up."

"Wouldn't have him around here if I were you," Sailor added with an eye toward me. "The boy might pick up some of his bad habits."

That's me by the way, or was: 'the boy' or 'Boy' if they were feeling personable.

It wasn't that I minded my job at the station. It was better than bagging groceries or hauling hay. But I hated working days. That's when Dad's friends came by to gossip. If I was lucky, they'd have one of their kids with them and we'd slip away to a corner somewhere. Mostly, though, I was on display, the dutiful son, to be seen and seen busy I might add— but most definitely not heard.

Just once I'd have liked to correct them. Nothing big, maybe just "My name is Tad" or something equally revolutionary. It wouldn't do any good though; I can hear Dad's "Hush!" even now.

Sailor was retired and had become a regular fixture around the station, leaving only for sustenance and then returning, sometimes for the day. One night, Dad and I were closing up before he finally left.

"Why do you let him hang around all day?" I asked as we drove home.

"Have some respect. Sailor Moon is a great man."

I should have known that was coming. Everyone in town knew Sailor was a decorated naval hero, hence the moniker: Sailor. The Moon part came from the location of an old battle wound. As Sailor would say, "Shrapnel caught me in the ass." I didn't even know his real name.

"I guess," I said, gratified Dad had deigned to discuss the matter, "but Dad, he's mean as hell."

"He's not mean at all, just tough. Oh, I know he grumbles a lot, and he likes to tease. But that's just how military men are."

"Well, all he does now is stand around all day and talk crap about people. You wouldn't let anyone else get away with that."

Dad's voice turned grave. "He's hurting son, and lonely now that his wife is gone. Would you really deny him a place to go and be with his friends?"

I shrugged.

"That would make you the mean one, wouldn't it?"

I breathed the kind of sigh perfected in adolescence. "I guess," I said and let it drop, for the moment anyway. Still, I just couldn't see the attraction. I mean women get a bad rap, on the gossip front, that is. But the guys at the station were worse than any women I ever knew. A stereotypical coffee klatch, if ever there was one. Sans the coffee.

I'd heard the rumors about Richie myself. That he'd gotten Susan pregnant. Everyone was shocked. Not so much about the sex. The shock, aside from the pregnancy, was Susan. Sure she was nice, and pretty, but not exactly an A-lister.

Susan's parents weren't happy about it, but Richie's Mom went clock-tower-bat-shit-crazy and threw him out. His dad, always kind of wimpy, just went along. The part nobody talked about was Richie forgoing college-ball to get a job and apartment for them to live.

Not juicy enough, I guess.

"Sleeping out there like a bum," Sailor growled. He grabbed one of the window-washer buckets I'd just filled. "This'll wake him up."

My hand locked around the handle so tight it spun Sailor back around. Our eyes locked.

I wanted to call him a hypocrite, a gossiping old biddy, nasty, ugly, bitter, and too many other things to list in polite company—I was fifteen, that's my excuse. Fifteen-year-olds didn't say things like that to friends of their fathers. Especially not to friends of *my* father, not if they wanted to see sixteen, anyway.

Sailor turned red and jerked the bucket. It barely moved. Something, not quite fear, but something registered behind his eyes, and he let the bucket go.

Dad walked to the Coke machine, dropped in a quarter, and punched Fanta Orange, Sailor's favorite, then handed him the can.

"Tad, would you go out and ask your friend to come in here a minute, I'd like to have a talk with him."

"Yes, sir," I said.

I walked outside on automatic pilot. *That didn't go so badly. All things considered, I shouldn't even be breathing.* The situation did not bode well for Richie though.

He wore the infamous leather vest, now scuffed and scarred, a Black Sabbath T-shirt beneath and filthy jeans, but no socks. His sneakers had holes over both big toes. The sole was beginning to rip from the shoe.

I opened my mouth to speak, but hesitated. True, school was out. Even so, high school hierarchy clearly forbade invisibles from initiating casual conversation with stars. It was during my hesitation that he awoke.

"Hey buddy," he said. "I didn't know you work here."

"Hey," I said. "Yeah, it's my Dad's place."

"Cool. Doing construction myself. Work sucks, but the pay's good." Suspicion crept into his eyes. "Do I have to leave? I mean, I will, of course I will, just... Susan has the car. Doing summer semester down at the college. I said I'd meet her here. Could you maybe ask your dad if I can hang 'til she gets here?"

"Sure... I mean, yeah I will, but he kind of sent me out to get you."

Just then Susan pulled up in a beat-up Pinto.

"Dude!" I blurted. "What happened to your car?"

"Sold it. Babies are expensive." Then he grinned. "Totally worth it though."

He greeted his Susan with a kiss. "Pull it over to the self-serve," he told her. "I've been here a while; we'd better get some gas."

"Can you tell your Dad I'll be right in?"

I nodded, headed back inside and shot Sailor a glare as I jabbed the *approve* button for the self-serve island. "He was waiting for his wife to pick him up," I said. "He'll be here in a minute."

A moment later, Richie walked in, not tentative, not defiant either, just confident, and handed Dad five bucks for the fuel.

"You wanted to see me, Mr. Benson?"

Dad took the money and walked to the register. "I did," he said, and pointed to a plaque on the wall. "Can you read that for me?"

It was just a silly old quote with a picture of a horse on it. So trivial that these days it would barely be good enough for a Facebook meme.

Richie dutifully recited the message. "If you treat your wife like a Thoroughbred, she'll never turn into an old nag." He chuckled, equally dutifully, it seemed to me.

Dad walked back with a hundred-dollar bill in his hand. "Don't use it for bills, gas, or diapers, or anything else I know you're going to need. I want you to take your beautiful bride out for a nice date. Often as you can, understand?"

Richie could only nod. Meanwhile, the rest of us developed a fascination with the floor.

"Now, I understand you need a place to wait for your wife. Why not come in next time?"

"Hell, yes," Sailor added. "We could use some new blood. The boy over there's so serious." Sailor pointed to me. "Boring as all get out."

Raincheck

J. Anthony Gohier

It's not that I don't want to see you.
I pine for late night walks through fields of fireflies
and rooftop views from island hostels I probably couldn't find again
if I tried

For the dancing in the rain
Until the thunder chased us inside,
And the tears spilled over thoughtless words
Spat between too many hours in the backseat of the same bus
And for the day-after apologies

But every time I turn to Facebook,
Hoping for a new adventure,
I find the pictures of me asleep in the backseat of your car
Have long since been replaced
By bridal veils wafting in soft breezes over salt flats,
And greyscale newborns snuggled in baby fat.

The midnight skinny-dipping in flooded rivers
Has been covered
In the fresh paint of picket fences,
And pictures of first-birthday cakes.
Pictures I'm still surprised not to see myself in.

Counting the days that have slipped away
Since the last time we sat on the roof outside your window
Envisioning all the things we'd be, and do, and have
When we finally grew up,
Realization congeals to acceptance
My everyday has become your remember when.

I know we said we'd never drift apart,
But you feel a little further
Every time I pick up the phone, and you ask me what's new
And I can't think of anything to say.

Within My Glass Box
Joni B. Haws

I AM AT CHURCH, but I don't want to be. Not because I am bored, or because I am dying to wriggle out of these nylons that make me feel like a cracked biscuit canister. Not because the air conditioning is controlled by the biggest guy in the room—wearing a three-piece suit—and my ankles are frosting over. No, I itch to leave the room, the oppressive stillness, to walk laps around the looped corridor surrounding the chapel, and mutter my frantic prayers in a soothing litany. Pray that with each step I can leave a grain of anxiety behind me in the office-grade teal carpet. Pray that the dissonance bubbling in my chest like pasta on a hot stove can ease.

Surrounded by people, I feel separate, like I am watching the world from inside a glass box, able only to hear the sluggish beats of my own heart. I glance around the chapel as the deacons in their too-short slacks pass the sacrament. It's the standard scene, a couple sitting close together, arms folded, a teenager resting his forehead on the pew before him, a young dad rummaging through a diaper bag for a binkie or fruit snacks. One little girl across the aisle lies on the floor lifting her dress above her head, wiggling tiny hips encased in Elsa undies. Her mother sits on the pew staring with unfocused eyes, her thoughts elsewhere.

I wonder if she's thinking about Jesus. Isn't that what we're supposed to do during the sacrament, think about Jesus? If that mom were paying attention to her toddler's flash-dance, she would likely tell her to put her dress down and think about Jesus. When my own kids misbehave during the sacrament service, I tell them to think about Jesus, even though I'm not exactly sure what I mean by it. Do I expect them to just repeat His name in their minds over and over? What does a seven-year-old really reflect upon when instructed to think about Jesus? They are empty words.

Empty like me. I watch us all sitting neatly in our box. When the bread reaches me, I take a piece, place it in my mouth, and dutifully pass the tray to Daren, who passes it along to our kids. I like getting the bread. It adds a little excitement to my meetings, not knowing exactly what we'll be getting. White? Wheat? Soft and fresh, or dry and crusty? You can tell when it is homemade, which doesn't happen much in this ward. We have settled into a WonderBread White phase. My children let their hands hover over the tray, scanning for the biggest and most crustless piece. Discerning, they are.

I look up at the men on the stand, our bishopric. Brother Bingham's head bobs momentarily, but he tugs an earlobe and muscles back the fatigue. Bishop Prows is attentive, his eyes scanning the congregation, his little flock. He's looking for lost sheep. But I know he won't find me, sixth row back, stage-left, aisle seat. I am as much a fixture of the room as the bench I sit on, having been in meetings like this one almost every week since birth. Not all who are lost wander.

Until they do. I wonder if I will miss it when I stop coming. My bargain with God is nearing its deadline, and though the scriptures tell me to have faith, I am still at a loss as to where to find it. If I *had* faith, I would have it. Where can I get some? That is the golden question. It has been seven days since I announced to Daren that I was conducting my own fast, a week ahead of our regularly-scheduled fast Sunday, and that I was fasting for hope.

"I don't need heavenly visitation or even a voice in my ear," I told him, "but I've got to know He's there. The turmoil is too much. I'm fasting for anything, really, that will let me know that I shouldn't leave." I am tired of the conflict that whorls inside me each Sunday as I teach children songs about love from a Heavenly Father, all the while unsure if I even believe them. "Some say that heaven is far away, but I feel it close around me as I pray," we sing, and the bitterness eats away at me behind my smile. I am tired of crying to God, waiting for that warm-hug feeling that never comes. "I will not leave you comfortless," the scriptures promise. I have either become an exception, or I have pinned hope on a promise that doesn't exist, maybe on a being that doesn't exist. If I am not righteous enough to receive The Comforter, then perhaps that level of righteousness isn't attainable. I'm so close to saying goodbye to all of this, Elsa undies notwithstanding.

Oh, I fasted. I burned with hunger, but not much more than that. I prayed to God, "Hey, Sir, I've been taught my whole life that fasting and prayer bring answers, so, this is me, fasting and praying. You've got to give me something. I'm dying down here." I waited all that day for the warm feeling, the bright thought, the call from the prophet. Nothing.

I gave God a deadline. This is inadvisable, as "trusting God also means trusting His timing," but my loneliness has spawned a reckless heart. As Primary Chorister, I have been teaching all the children of the congregation a series of songs to be performed during sacrament meeting at the end of the month. I have told God, and, tearfully, my husband, that if something doesn't change for me by the time we present the Primary Program, I will ask to be released and begin my church hiatus. An indefinite hiatus. The dropping of that stone will cast a heavy wake, but something has to give.

I have been officially diagnosed with Major Depressive Disorder for over a decade, and struggling with its effects for more than two. I am messed up, but that's what the Atonement is for, right? Christ is my friend, ready and willing to take my burdens upon Him. Only, I can't seem to get anyone to explain the practical application of how, exactly, they are to be transferred. And they are getting heavy. The little beast I carry inside me is mine to keep, and sometimes he gets vocal. Though I understand that his whispers and shouts of self-loathing, hatred, panic, and guilt are lies, they feel like the most apparent truths, and when he speaks I am powerless but to listen. I have been waiting for God to counteract the beast with light, to fight the lies with the truth of my divine worth. I have been taught the pattern since my youth. You pray for help and God helps you. I feel like a kid with an empty stocking on Christmas, not even coal. There is nothing.

The sacrament ends and it is time for the bearing of testimonies. Sister Dunford minces to the stand, her back surgery still healing, and proclaims her faith in God's awareness of her, that He cares so much about the minutia of her life He helped her find a misplaced gift for her grandson. I like Sister Dunford, her gentle voice and ladylike posture. She plays the piano in Primary, and sometimes when I drop by her house with the list of songs to practice for that month she has fat curlers in her blonde bob. Good for you, Tracy. I don't resent her for getting such a simple and immediate answer to her prayers, but it does hurt. I don't doubt that she would score higher on the righteousness scale, if righteousness were indeed weighted by checklist items, but I have believed in a God whose grace is sufficient for all. Don't I fit under the umbrella? Maybe she just found the gift because she looked harder after she prayed. Maybe no one was actually listening. How can a just deity care about the location of a gift-wrapped toy over my desperate need to know such a deity even exists?

I've had this internal debate so many times it has worn a groove in my brain. I've been raised in a faith that promotes learning truth for yourself through feeling, the confirmation of the Holy Spirit, the still small voice. Each person is entitled to personal revelation, a testimony built upon an individual relationship with God. If we earnestly seek after Him, we will feel Him, and it will strengthen us, build our faith.

But my emotions are not to be trusted, leaving my faith in a confusing limbo. I know that much of the time the feelings in my heart are utterly contrary to what I have been taught about myself as a daughter of Heavenly Parents who love me. What to do with tear-muddied prayers that leave me with nothing but the compulsion to escape from this life? How to proceed when my searching of the scriptures only reveals to me ever deeper levels of personal failure? Lately my study has produced deep, loathsome feelings that sit like rocks in my gut.

But at least Sister Dunford found her present.

No, I won't miss this feeling, the ripping pull of what I am supposed to feel against my actual feelings. I don't fit into this box, and I can't pretend anymore. I snake my fingers into Daren's and stare across the laps of my little family. The kids share the crayons between them as they look for the right pictures to color in their books. Teia likes to make dark sweeps of color just inside the lines before shading in the rest of the spaces, a technique I taught her. She's so much like Daren, taking comfort in doing things the prescribed way. Choosing the right. I have anguished over how my decision will hurt and confuse my kids, and I will certainly anguish more, but at the moment I feel placid enough.

A young woman swishes past me in the aisle and makes a smooth ascent to the microphone. Her hair falls in a blonde curtain over one shoulder. Looking like a lovely wedding centerpiece in a pastel chiffon blouse and creamy cardigan, she exudes the type of feminine charm I have never tracked down in myself. I scratch my arm with a naked, blunt fingernail as she takes a deep breath, acknowledging that she is not a member of our ward, but felt compelled to stand and speak about a subject that she finds difficult. Her manicured hands grip the podium on either side.

"For the last three years I've struggled deeply with Depression. It's been very hard on me, and on my faith, because when you're depressed you can't feel the Spirit."

I make an audible gasp. Like an airbag expanding upon impact, my chest fills with emotion, tears all but leaping from my eyes. I drown in the feeling before I can even register it. My heart feels like it might rattle free from its cage as she continues to speak. For years, she has not felt God, but recognizes now that she has never been left without an angel. Even when she felt most alone, she had hands of family or friends to hold her in the darkness. My crying progresses into hiccoughing sobs and I lean forward, resting my forehead on Daren's knee. I am nudging the boundary of causing a scene.

The words of that twenty-something stranger speak the language of my heart, a spell invoking buried things to rise. There are still, and may always be, tough questions for which I have no answers, but her shaking voice reflects back to me the same phrases I used in my yearning ultimatum to God. They refract my dim light and turn me to fire inside a suit of trembling, croaking flesh. This young beauty is my sister, the mirror of my heart. In that moment, the pretty girl with the smooth hair is God standing outside my glass box of silence, bouncing about and waving His arms, mouthing the words, "I am here."

A War to Bring Peace
Krystal Gerber

"Pepper Jack cheese!" Mr. Harris bellowed, thumping the arm of his armchair. "Pepper Jack cheese, darn it all!"

Sparkplug looked up at his master from his cushion in the corner. Sparkplug was a black Labrador, had never been called Sparky in his life, and had never attempted anything exciting since the puppyish day he'd licked the outlet and earned his name. His owner had never done anything exciting at all, which is why Sparkplug raised his head when Mr. Harris raised his voice at the television.

"No, I'm afraid the answer was 'Pepper Jack', or 'Pepper Jack cheese'." Alex Trebek's polite words and the crowd's televised moans were swallowed up in the tiny living room packed with dustless mementos.

"Ach!" Mr. Harris slapped the armchair again, and lurched up out of his seat and into the equally tiny kitchen, pausing to straighten a photo frame of his dead wife that was a hair out of place. Glancing out the window, he glared at the scroungy, gray tomcat lounging on his porch rail. The filthy stray, which looked like it had won many fights and lost even more, seemed to mock Harris with its golden eyes narrowed to slits.

"Off!" Mr. Harris shouted, waving one hand. "Off, you flea-bitten thing!"

Sparkplug didn't look up at this. His master often yelled at the stray cat.

The cat didn't look up either. After glaring unflappably back at Mr. Harris, he lazily got to his feet, licked a paw to make it clear it was all *his* idea, and scampered off the porch.

Mr. Harris promptly forgot the cat, shuffling towards his pantry and muttering, "The category was American Made, 'a cousin to Monterey Jack cheese'. Bumbling idiots! The lot of them!"

Still muttering, Mr. Harris pulled out a new loaf of whole-wheat bread, thinking darkly about cheeses, Jeopardy contestants, and stray cats guilty of making yellow spots on his lawn. With a grumble, he cut into the loaf, chewing on his mustache.

For a moment, he thought he was finally going senile. The knife jerked oddly, as if he were cutting through air, and the bread loaf fell apart. Goggling, Mr. Harris creakily leaned over, eyeing the loaf in disbelief.

Something, *something* had hollowed out the whole center of his brand-new loaf. It smelled like his bathroom sink that he couldn't afford to fix—musty and acrid. There were little grains scattered inside the bread too, black and oblong.

Mr. Harris scowled at the little grains. He bought *whole* wheat bread—whole wheat. None of that new-age, hipster bread for *him*. Those weren't grains at all they were—*droppings*.

"Mouse," Harris whispered, his mustache trembling in fury. Fury wasn't something Harris was accustomed to feeling. Nothing but Jeopardy and that mangy cat managed to raise his blood pressure—he wouldn't allow it. He dusted every other day and vacuumed on Tuesdays—*every* Tuesday. His pantry was alphabetized. Yet somehow the Mouse had snuck into the Bs, and eaten his way into a new doughy RV—with breakfast in bed!

Mr. Harris slid the loaf jerkily into the trash, glancing darkly at the pantry. For just a moment, he felt like a scheming general as he bent slowly over to fish underneath his sink for his Weapons of Mouse Destruction.

By the next day, Sparkplug didn't dare stick so much as his nose in the pantry, let alone his whole tongue. Bristling with shiny snap traps, the floor was an impassable mousy-minefield, with open boxes of sickly blue mouse poison stuffed behind the raspberry jam.

Smugly, Mr. Harris went back to sit in his old armchair, the cushions formed to his shape from sheer repetition. He waited, taking his handful of pills and watching Home Shopping Network. He waited as he ate his bland scrambled eggs, the same breakfast he'd had for twenty years. He waited as day turned to dusk and Wheel of Fortune came on, slurping his sodium-free canned soup, one eye on the pantry door.

There was no panicked squeaking. There was no raucous snapping. At last, Mr. Harris went to bed, feeling defeated.

He awoke at midnight, an odd occurrence for him. Mr. Harris did not like anything odd. Nervously, he got out of bed, checking the locks. Just in case. Then, he shuffled in to take a peek at the pantry—just in case.

He left the lights off, knowing the house too well to need them. Yet as he stepped onto the old linoleum, he heard an odd sound. Scrabbling. Scratching.

Jerking the refrigerator open, Mr. Harris flooded the kitchen and pantry with light. Quickly, he peered inside, hoping to see a flailing mouse.

What he saw made his blood run chilly in his veins, and his heart pump faster than was healthy.

One beady, shining eye glowed from behind the peanut butter jar. Its black, cold gaze was fixed on him, *him,* as quickly the owner of the terrible eye darted out onto the open shelf.

Skirting blithely past the snap traps, the Mouse—for Mr. Harris knew this terrifying creature must be *the* Mouse—scrabbled its way quickly from the middle shelf to the bottom shelf, feet moving quick as lightning. Where the Mouse had lost its other eye, Mr. Harris couldn't begin to guess, but he knew one thing. This was no ordinary foe.

With laughable ease, the fat mouse skittered past the Yawning Traps of Metallic Death as Mr. Harris privately thought of them. The Mouse turned up his whiskers at the blue poison, and scampered right to the prunes, darting into the box, his tail hanging out like a stuck-out tongue.

A sort of horror consumed Mr. Harris at the sight. In helpless panic, he eyed the floor mat of mousetraps, his own barricade turned against him, the rustling sound from the prune box making him angrier with every passing moment.

Furiously, Mr. Harris went back to his stash of anti-mouse weaponry. Leaning precariously over the glittering floor, he layered the shelves with glue traps, his entire stash laid out until the whole of Mr. Harris's government-paid house reeked of the sticky stuff. The tail had disappeared, and the prune box was effectively surrounded by a carpet of gummy death.

Going to bed that morning—for it was morning by now, even if the sun had yet to come up—Harris couldn't close his eyes without seeing a beady-eyed Mouse, couldn't roll over in bed without hearing again the sound of little teeth chewing into his box of prunes. It made his old soul shiver, made him afraid to stick a toe out from beneath the covers. He barely slept, yet habit forced him to stay in bed until eight o'clock, sweating. Wondering.

Finally, he rose. In his flannels, he snuck into the silent kitchen, creeping towards the pantry. Tremulously, he reached out to open the door.

Ghosting past the glue traps laid down thick as rugs in a Persian parlor, the Mouse sniffed along the middle shelf. Starting towards the door, the Mouse climbed across the tops of the boxed rice, so neatly and tightly packed together into an elevated mouse freeway.

Heart thumping wildly, Mr. Harris slammed the door and quickly grabbed the first thing that met his fingers when he reached under the sink for reinforcements—duct tape. Frantically, Mr. Harris slapped a strip of duct tape all along the bottom of the pantry door, blocking any exit.

This was, remarkably, not the dumbest thing ever done in the quest for pest control. However, it was *nearly* the dumbest thing, which Mr. Harris realized the moment after he'd done it.

"Like locking Jesse James in a bank," he mumbled in disgust, rising slowly to his feet and carefully putting the duct tape away in the proper place .

Yet after he'd finished, Mr. Harris paused, leaning heavily against the wall, still shaking from the encounter. It had been stupid, sure. But maybe there was a plot lurking in this latest stupidity—maybe there was a way to end the war, once and for all.

For two days, Mr. Harris prepared his Last Stand. As every good general knows, when overt tactics fail, siege warfare takes over. Digging two old bins out of the closet, Mr. Harris dumped the dusty Christmas tinsel and half-burnt-out lights onto the floor and dragged the bins to the pantry. He grabbed trash bags out from under the sink as Sparkplug watched from his cushion, withholding judgment.

The next morning, with trepidation like cement around his heart, Harris shuffled to the pantry, brandishing his broom like a saber. He watched the pantry door, feeling as he imagined Wellington had felt facing Napoleon's front line. With trembling fingers, he bent, ripped away the duct tape and wildly swung the door open.

He couldn't see the Mouse, but he knew the enemy was there, hiding behind the boxes of Hamburger Helper like a little furry guerrilla. He knew the Mouse had been feasting off its enemy's rations, getting fatter and smugger. Yet all that was about to change.

First, Mr. Harris swept away the mousetraps on the floor, flinching as they snapped against the broom. Then, with a tortured grimace, Mr. Harris started scooping packages into the empty bins. With huge sweeps of his arm, he tore his carefully labelled and alphabetized items off the shelves and tumbled them haphazardly into the bin. Heart beating painfully fast, Harris cleaned off the bottom and middle shelves. With trembling in his hands and murder in his heart, he climbed onto his stepladder and reached for the top shelf.

As he rose higher, one beady eye came level with his, appearing behind the spices like a sniper in the brush.

The sight of the foe had a terrible effect. Madness rose in Mr. Harris's heart and he reached out, sweeping his arm like the Angel of Death, spices flying like shrapnel into the air.

What he had never expected was how wily a mouse with one eye had to be to go on thieving. The Mouse didn't hide—he didn't run. He leapt off the shelf and straight into Harris' wrinkled, livid face.

Whatever anger Mr. Harris felt evaporated into terror. Staggering back, he fell off the step-ladder and against the shelves, the narrowness of the pantry just saving him from breaking a hip. Yet the Mouse kept flying, out of the pantry and into the kitchen, streaking towards freedom.

Mr. Harris, filled with blood-lust, grabbed the broom and shuffled after him almost at a run. Slam! Slam! Slam! Harris whacked at the floor, shrieking like a madman, chasing the Mouse through the kitchen and towards the front door. Scrambling for its life, the Mouse tore across the faded carpet, squeaking furiously, tail whipping as it took tight hold of the window curtains and tore towards the ceiling.

Twisting round like Babe Ruth at the plate, Harris swung with all the strength of a desperate and persecuted man, hitting the curtains a sideways blow and knocking the mouse free.

History turns on small hinges, and in wars with mice, sometimes tiny things loom the largest. Perhaps the fact the window was open a crack wouldn't have mattered in the scheme of history, but in a war with a quadruped, nothing could have been more disastrous.

Squeaking in triumph, the Mouse squeezed through the opening, and disappeared over the windowsill. Yet it stopped on the edge and looked back at Mr. Harris, a special gleam in its eye.

Mr. Harris knew what the gleam meant, as if the Mouse had shouted at him. *I'll be back. I have my special hole, my entrance to your humble home. This war has not ended, oh no. Winter will come, and I know where your loaf of bread is. I'll haunt your home and torture your dreams, and now you know you can't stop me.*

In despair, Mr. Harris watched the Mouse scamper off the sill and onto the porch. Jerkily, he yanked open the door, hoping to do something—anything—to keep the Mouse from keeping its terrible promise.

Then suddenly, the Mouse took off, a terrified streak towards the open door—straight towards Mr. Harris!

Harris staggered back, let out a little yelp—and stared in disbelief as a gray streak shot up behind the Mouse and caught it in his jaws just short of the door. Scraggly, missing bits of his ear, disreputable as ever, the gray tom chewed away at the Mouse, swallowing it in four quick bites. Sitting up, he licked his lips in satisfaction, the Mouse, the archenemy, now only a tasty memory.

As the cat ate, Mr. Harris gawked, wondering if he was having a heart attack—or hallucinating. When it had finished, the cat fluffed up, as if realizing who was standing in the doorway. It hissed a warning and scampered away, totally unconscious of the war it had so enjoyed ending.

Habit won out over his shock, and Mr. Harris waved a hand angrily at the cat as it ran off, gasping breathlessly, "Out! Out, you ratty thing!"

Mr. Harris watched the cat go, gripping the doorframe feebly, the toll of his murderous charge making him wilt where he stood. Glancing back at the nearly-empty pantry, Harris felt even emptier himself.

Sparkplug whined softly, sensing his owner's mood. Lurching up from his pillow, he stuck his nose into the old man's hand, but the hand didn't pat him as Mr. Harris turned, closed the door, and shuffled back to his chair.

Slowly, Mr. Harris put his systematic life back together. He ate his scrambled eggs the next morning and rebuilt his pantry, though he shuddered as he lifted Hamburger Helper onto the shelves, seeing beady eyes behind every jar of raspberry jam.

That night, as he warmed up his soup he glanced out the window and saw the old scroungy cat on his front porch rail. For a long minute, Harris stared at the cat, and then he looked away, carrying the soup to his chair to watch Wheel of Fortune. Yet Harris didn't start eating. He didn't yell the answer. Not this time.

He glanced up at the photo of his wife, gone for so long—enough years that he couldn't remember exactly how many.

"She loved cats, Sparkplug," Harris muttered, staring at Vanna White without really seeing her. "She loved kittens especially. You wouldn't have gotten along with her, my boy. And she always paid her debts. Eh?"

Sparkplug raised his brows, but didn't answer back. Yet he noticed a change in his owner after that night. Afterwards, once a week, his owner did something odd. Something that made Sparkplug look up.

Every Tuesday, Mr. Harris stuck with his usual routine, vacuuming the house and watching Jeopardy. However, just as Alex Trebek said goodbye, Harris lurched from his seat and turned off his TV. Shuffling to his fridge for a carton, he grabbed a plastic bowl and headed to the front door.

Sparkplug looked up in interest every Tuesday as Mr. Harris unlocked the door, stepped outside, and poured a generous portion of milk into the cheap bowl. Then he set the bowl on the rail and stepped back inside.

Yet he didn't go back to his chair. Oddly enough, Mr. Harris stood and waited behind the window. And every Tuesday a scroungy, gray cat climbed onto the railing, licked his fuzzy lips and lapped up the milk with the air of a king at Sunday brunch.

And every Tuesday Mr. Harris watched him fondly, smiling.

Pineapple Rules
Pam Tucker

Pompous little package
in brocaded peacockery
shock top green
all punk and prance
hula-cool ruler
on a high horse
lording it over
a swale of pale bananas

whack smack deposed
in violent coup
crown toppled
cocksure prince
shucked, knife-sliced
disrobed flesh
left to stare down
the end of a sharp stick

skewered, grilled
silver-tongued
high-heat huckster
every last tidbit
urging proletarian peppers
and chicken-lickin' lowlife
to *Rise up, Rise up*
follow you to your
next kingdom come

Fishing with Heber Stock
Kathy Davidson

BEAR LAKE LIES across the border between Utah and Idaho. It has the most beautiful blue waters seen this side of the Caribbean. Most people know it as a paradise of the Rockies. I grew up in a village on the Bear Lake shore.

The lake serves all kinds of people. The farmers downstream use it to store water for their crops. The depths are great for training scuba divers. The swimmers and water skiers love the shallow beaches. Then there are the fishermen. This is my group. There are four breeds of fish that are found no other place on earth; Bonneville Cisco, Bear Lake Whitefish, Bear Lake Sculpin and the Bonneville Whitefish. The Cisco is a small greasy fish mostly used for bait.

What I remember best about growing up near Bear Lake is Heber Stock, our next-door neighbor. Heber was old when I was three. He was withered and bowlegged. His back was so bent he couldn't stand up straight and still he had to duck when he went through the doorways of his house. He was so old he lived before there were cars and rode horses everywhere. He built a house for his bride by cutting trees on the mountains and dragging them to town behind a horse. He was a cowboy and he was my hero. I wanted to be like him when I grew up. He had adventures most people only read about. I loved to sit and listen to the stories about his life. It was better than reading Zane Gray.

When I knew him, Heber spent most of his time fishing. He would go every day, rain or shine, winter or summer. He loved living by the lake and knew everything about it. When he wasn't fishing he worked in his garden.

He told me it was the minerals in the water that reflected the color of the sky. In the morning the lake is a silver color, reflecting the new sun-- it appears to glow. In the afternoon the lake is the most perfect turquoise blue. Heber taught me the deepest part of the lake, near two hundred feet deep, reflected the darkest blues. The shallow shores don't reflect the blue as well and look glassy. Heber taught me about the wind picking up in the afternoons and making the lake downright dangerous. That's one of the reasons Heber only fished in the mornings and spent his afternoons in the garden. Otherwise, he would be out on the lake all day.

In the early afternoons when my chores were done, or whenever I could escape the work, I loved to climb through the fence and visit with Heber while he worked in his garden. Heber showed me mole holes under his carrots and the eggs in the bird's nest in his apple trees. He also told me about his fishing trips. They seemed magical. More than anything I wanted to go fishing on Bear Lake with him.

The morning my father announced we were going ice fishing with Heber was the best day of my life. I packed up my warm clothes and got ready for amazing adventures we were about to have.

Heber once told me about the time he and his buddy Don went ice fishing. Don had worked in the mines and was on oxygen. He wheezed as he breathed, sounding like Darth Vader. His ever-present oxygen tank didn't seem to bother Heber. They had been friends since the old days. Heber would pack Don, the portable oxygen tank, food, and the fishing gear into a sled he could pull behind his snowmobile and they would be off for a day on the lake. The ice was only thick in spots that year, so they went on the south end, near Laketown where the ice was thicker. After a fun filled day of fishing, they repacked everything on top of Don in the sled, Heber started up the machine, and they headed home. They hadn't gone far when they found the ice had floated, creating a twenty-foot gap of open water. By the time

Heber noticed the gap, it was too late to turn around. He did the only thing he knew, he gunned it. The snowmobile skidded across the water, dragging Don in the sled behind to get to the ice on the other side of the gap.

I asked him if he was afraid Don might have drowned. He said, "Na, he had his oxygen."

I laughed and couldn't wait to experience the adventure myself.

We loaded our gear onto the ice and drilled a hole. Then I waited. When was the adventure going to start? I watched the ice close to see if it would float us away. I nearly jumped out of my skin when the ice moaned. I whooped when a thundering crack sliced by. Heber didn't even look up. I understand now my father would never agree to go fishing if the ice wasn't two feet deep over the entire lake. We did a lot of sitting-- a lot of it. We only caught three fish and one of them was less than the legal length to keep. It was nothing to brag about. I was so disappointed I didn't beg to go ice fishing again. I thought maybe summer fishing would be more of an adventure.

Heber had so many stories about fishing in a boat. He once told me about a time he took the Utah Fish and Game wardens fishing. They needed help checking the fish population. Heber met them on Cisco Beach on the east side of the lake, Utah side. They went out in the state boat. It's a nice one, big enough to rescue tourists in rough waters. Heber agreed to go just so he could enjoy the luxury boat. He told them to go above Rock Pile. The bottom of the lake at this spot is covered with porous rock instead of sand. The little fish like to hide there, so many bigger fish hunt there. This was where Heber snagged a little rock that looks like a rocking sea horse.

He had to stop his story and show the rock to me. He kept it on the windowsill by his back door. If I used my imagination a little, I could see the seahorse and its base isn't flat, so it does rock. I was impressed.

Well, Heber was fishing with the wardens and he got a bite. It was a big one. One of the wardens grabbed the net and helped get the fish into the boat. Heber watched as they examined the fish, measured the length and weight, pinned a tag on and threw it back.

Heber looked at me with his shocked face. His big old face looked bigger and his mouth hung open. "Can you believe those daggum wardens threw my fish back!" His eyes wide, he looked at me until I was indignant enough for him. "I had to watch one of the biggest fish I've ever caught swim away. I almost jumped in to go after it."

I had seen many of his large fish. He even had one mounted on his wall. So, I imagined it was maybe even bigger than I was.

Well, he said he mumbled a few choice words under his breath. He didn't tell me the words, just let me use my imagination. The wardens chuckled and went back to their own lines. Heber said he grumped for a while until the wardens got him a soda and all was forgiven--until the next fish was caught. Heber was shocked to see the same thing happen again. The warden grabbed the net, the fish, weight, length, tag, and back into the water. This time Heber said he didn't just mumble those words. He turned his back on the wardens and wouldn't talk to them. They tried to laugh it off, but Heber wasn't having it. The next fish Heber caught on his line, he was going to take home to his wife. The wardens agreed to let him. It wasn't as big as the first fish he caught, in fact it was barely big enough to legally keep, but the wardens agreed Heber had earned it and let him keep his catch.

I wanted to fish and catch three fish I could keep. I wanted to be able to tell my friends about the big fish Heber would help me catch. The day finally came the next summer. My dad and I went fishing with Heber. It was another boring day. I didn't catch anything. I watched Heber catch a fish. He didn't even use a pole. Instead he slipped a line over his finger and bobbed it up and down in the water. I tried it myself, but the line cut my finger. It burned like a paper cut. I sucked on it for a minute as Heber showed the calluses he had developed on his finger from years of fishing without a pole.

Heber took us to the east side of the lake and showed us the bank where the mountain drops steep into the water. The park service had sunk some cars to keep the bank from eroding. The scuba divers like to use this beach for training. Because of the lake's high elevation, a scuba diver can certify for deep water, without going deep. It brings good business to the people around lake.

Heber told us another story as we sat bobbing our poles in the water. He was fishing with Don and another friend Evan. Evan is the young one of the famous trio. He retired early because of his bad heart.

Heber and the boys (he called them boys, but they were older than my grandpa) put out their lines and sat watching the divers come in and out of the water. The fish weren't biting and the boys were getting too much sun, so Heber decided to give up for the day. They left their lines in as they motored to shore. Evan, with his bad heart, was elected to watch the lines as Don helped Heber load the gear and the boat in the back of the truck. When they had just about finished loading, Evan yelled out, "Heber's line has a tug." Heber rushed over and started fighting the fish. It was a strong fighter, and he'd figured he caught a real big one this time. The two struggled, in and out, the fish winning, then Heber winning, then the fish took out more line. Heber worked the line careful so it wouldn't break. He didn't want to lose the fish or his favorite lure. They continued to fight, in and out. After about thirty minutes the line went still. Heber tugged. It wouldn't give. It was stuck somewhere. The fish wasn't pulling out either. Somewhere between the fish and Heber the line was caught. Don suggested maybe one of the divers could go down and unsnag the line and perhaps bring the fish in. Evan volunteered to ask and soon found a willing diver to go see what was going on down there. The three friends waited for what seemed like an hour, but was probably only fifteen minutes before the diver came back to the surface.

"There's a car down there and the fish is inside," he told Heber. "The window isn't open enough for me to reach in."

Heber and the boys were at a loss. They didn't want to go home empty-handed or without Heber's favorite lure. So, they had this idea to send down a gaff hook with the diver to stab the fish and bring it back. One of the other divers had one and sent it back down to get the fish. The diver was gone even longer this time. Heber felt his line loosen and figured it's been cut. They got excited to see the big fish. But the diver came up empty handed.

"What happened? Where's my fish?" Heber demanded of the diver.

"Sorry, I tried. Every time I reached in to get the fish, he rolled the window up further."

Dad chuckled, and I realized the fish really didn't do that. I was disappointed again. My dad told me it was just a story and most all fishing trips are just about sitting and enjoying the quiet lake and thinking up stories to tell. He said I must not be old enough to appreciate it yet.

Well, I got old enough to appreciate it. I don't get the luxury to enjoy fishing on the calm waters of Bear Lake as often as I would like. But, I do think up stories to tell. They aren't as wild as Heber's or always about fishing. I love telling them though. Making my face all long with my mouth hanging open or motioning the way he did when he caught the big one. I guess in a way, I grew up to be like Heber Stock after all. My life is as exciting as a Zane Gray novel—in my imagination.

The 105
Daniel Cureton

The flame rose higher
And the sound of heat, gushed.
The button was pushed with eyer
As the closed door shut, hushed.

The leaves unfold
As the paper burned.
And the crisping sound untold
through the centuries traveled, learned

A simple herbological specimen
arrived in the collection of Louis XIII.
But kept from Australia 200 years as dead men
Do keep their secrets, grave born still, 19th.

What Labillardière gathered so carefully
survived through the Revolution's aim.
The World Horrors of 20th Century passing merrily
yet, be so tossed into the consuming delights of flame.

Jardin des Plantes,
Tagged, boxed, shipped from bureau
Muséum National d'Histoire Naturelle, France.
Colhelper, No 71250:

Tony Bean, botanist,
Queensland Herbarium, Australia.
Asking des Plantes "where is my catalyst?"
the government answered sesquipedalia.

Olearia, flowering plant, Asteraceae family
Daisies and sunflowers alike.
To identify and classify, happily
Seed, stem, leaves, and pit to strike.

In the notes of a book now closed
the package of Australian history, embers.
In the oven of biosecurity, disposed
the job done, security officers unhindered.

The only comfort to centuries of dead gone by
an email, no sugar, no feeling.
Government empathy, thought, and lies
fingered the send button, bureaucrat's willing.

References

O'Malley, Nick. "Would you burn the Mona Lisa if it was sent?': Our horror bureaucratic bungle." *The Sunday Morning Herald*, Lifestyle, 23 Feb, 2018. https://www.smh.com.au/lifestyle/would-you-burn-the-mona-lisa-if-it-was-sent-our-horror-bureaucratic-bungle-20180213-h0w0w3.html. Accessed 28 Feb 2018.

The Telling of the Bees
Katharine P. Goodman

I sense a change of seasons coming,
Winter's parting kiss was numbing,
There is a new stillness in the wind,
I understand I'm losing my old friend,
Because the bees have started humming.

Things are more enchanting in the spring,
When passion flows through everything,
Winter's adieu brings a bitter rend,
I sense a change.

Life cycles a continual wellspring,
Each season brings a new beginning,
"Despair Not" is the song the bees send,
It's a chorus about life that never ends.
So too, our voices should be singing,
I sense a change.

What Are You Living For?
Samantha Thorup

THERE'S ONE QUESTION I hate above all other questions.

"Do you have kids?"

I never know how to answer that. It should be a simple yes or no, but not for me. Should I tell them about my angel baby? Should I even tell people about Tristan? Should I tell them he's dead?

I wasn't always this way. As it often happens, seasons of my life shaped me, refined me through both bitter and moving experiences. If only you knew who I was before—but now I'm thinking about this question too much.

I don't want to think about that question. Instead, I think about a question that has been stirring inside of me. Above all the others I could ask, this is the one that rises to the top.

What are you living for?

Some people say that the basis of life is purpose, driving toward something, a greater meaning. Others say it comes from understanding who you are and where you came from. These are questions human beings have asked since the beginning of time.

But if you were to answer, what are you living for? That is a question worth answering.

Before

I gasp for breath. Again. Close my eyes. Breathe.

Nine months of training, but starting out, I am already exhausted. This is not good. I want to look at the other swimmers around me, but my vision is blurry. Bear Lake is warm, even in September, but that's not the problem.

The problem is I can see the bottom of the lake and that really freaks me out. I definitely can't touch the bottom.

I know I'm not afraid of heights, but now I know that I *am* afraid of deep water.

I flip onto my back, stroking. When I signed up for this sprint triathlon, I knew swimming would be the hardest part. Being under five feet tall is not an advantage for swimming long distances.

It's only 750 meters, I think to myself, but my backstroke is struggling. Okay, *I'm* struggling.

Groaning to myself, I try to remember why I signed up for this in the first place. The answer comes to me instantly. This is who I am. I enjoy challenges. People know me as the girl who ran her own business, managing 100 sales reps at age 19. I am the girl that isn't great at sewing or cooking but I *am* great at overcoming challenges.

Today, I will do this. I will prove myself.

I am by far the last girl to finish the swim in my category. At this point, however, I'm so relieved I don't even stop to beat myself up over it. I run towards my bike, unzip my wet suit and begin to pedal.

This part is easier. I can breathe again. I can do this.

I grit my teeth as I push my legs.

My only saving grace is passing my husband on the bike. We've been married over two years now. I never thought I'd get married at 20 but when people meet him, they understand. Over six feet tall, with blue eyes and dashing good looks. He waves at me, a huge smile lighting his face. He's always been the lighthearted, easygoing one and it shows. He makes this look easy.

I can't help but grin back. This gives me the energy I need to finish the 12-mile bike ride.

I hardly remember getting off the bike and running the last three miles. My legs feel like jelly from the transition of pedaling to running.

I do remember the finish line, overcome with relief. I did it! I knew I could, but there's a thought nagging at the back of my mind.

Why was it so hard after all my training?

At this time, I'm living for the glory, but even then—I still feel like something's missing.

During

I'm pregnant.

Not even a week after the sprint triathlon, I had this funny feeling. Because of that, I took a pregnancy test. I know I will always remember September 19th, 2015. It's engraved in my mind.

It all makes sense now and I'm almost relieved to get this news. So *that's* why it was so hard for me to swim. And bike. And run. Much harder than my training sessions. No wonder I was so tired last week.

I look at Mike, laughing because he's holding in his hands not one, but *three* pregnancy tests. He didn't believe me at first, but he sure does now.

He's ecstatic. I don't fight it. I let myself feel happy, excited. This wasn't in my plan, not by a long shot. I'm going to be a mom sooner than I thought.

But I couldn't be happier about it.

I can't believe how fast the months pass. . We tell my parents the weekend of my mom's birthday on September 30th, 2015. There's an instant eruption of anticipation, shouting and hugging. It's almost enough to help me forget my morning sickness—almost.

I've always been prone to nausea and I can't believe I actually lose weight in my first trimester.

On October 19, 2015, I hear the baby's heartbeat for the first time. So, the morning sickness is worth it, after all.

When we find out it's a boy on December 6th, 2015, I'm in shock. I really thought it was a girl, but my heart immediately warms to the idea.

I feel an instant connection with my son. I talk to him all the time about everything—how worried I am that I'll get bored staying at home, how excited I am to spend time with him, how he *must* be my son because I keep craving fries at three in the morning.

The second trimester is golden. I finally start showing a tiny baby bump around the end of February.

Mike and I didn't even have to think about a name. He's going to be Tristan.

It's evident throughout the third trimester that Tristan understands me. I don't know how he does, but he does. He kicks when I am upset and moves when I am happy. No matter what, he *always* kicks for Daddy.

I'm really not that surprised when I go into labor on April 22nd, 2016—almost four weeks early. Of *course* he would come the day I'm graduating college.

It's not like any labor I've ever heard of. My water broke, but it's leaking really slowly instead of gushing. I can feel contractions but they mostly feel like menstrual cramps.

Within six hours, I'm holding him. I hardly even had to push.

Maybe that's why he's so perfect.

I've changed my mind. I'm living for him.

I never knew life could be this great. I'm not really doing much by anyone else's standards. When I pictured myself at this age, I thought I'd be traveling the world and making loads of money, running several businesses or something. But I'm not doing any of that.

In fact, I am so tired, I don't want to think about traveling or being productive.

It's 1:00 a.m., after all, and it's just Tristan and me. Mike is beside us but he's got work and school tomorrow so I let him sleep. I've finally got Tristan on a good sleeping schedule. It's been three weeks, and we've got a good rhythm. He still has to feed every three hours. Everyone says he needs to grow because he's so tiny.

Secretly, I love that he's only about six pounds. He takes after his momma. I know he needs to grow but I *love* how little he is. After all, sometimes it's the small things that matter.

I giggle as Tristan struggles to eat. He gives me his scrunchy face.

"Don't be like that, son," I say, smiling. "Momma's got you."

I've just gotten to sleep again when I hear the alarm go off at 4:00 a.m. to feed him. My eyes are heavy, but I've got Netflix and best of all, Tristan is feeling extra cuddly.

I can't get over how great being a mom is. My own mom always talks about how amazing it is to love her six kids. She told me that our hearts manage to expand as our capacity for love grows.

What is inexplicable is not how much I love having a baby or being a mom.

I can't explain how much I love *him*.

As we go throughout our day, Tristan is just … Tristan. He is one of the quirkiest babies I know. Every time I go to feed or change him, he makes this face like he's trying to whistle. His eyes are always watching me, as though he actually knows what I'm going through.

Then he'll spit up on me so I know he's still a baby.

As I'm getting ready, someone texts me and asks if they can come see my baby. I say yes because honestly? I need a break and Tristan is always an angel around other people.

I decide to go on a walk before they come over. Our stroller was a gift from people in our neighborhood and it's way too big for this little man. He's content to just stay inside. I make sure to wrap him so that he's warm and so the sun won't shine in his face.

I'm rocking the mom look today. No makeup. Sweats. But I really don't mind because after our walk, Tristan wants to be on his favorite place: my chest.

I love that he's taken to this. This boy is so snuggly and sweet.

That doesn't stop me from taking a nap when my friend comes over. I get the benefit of sharing him and she fawns over him. As always, he hardly cries. He really is perfect. Most people are drawn to his warmth and his beautiful eyes.

Something about him carries so much depth and yet—he's still quirky. Sometimes I wonder if he's better at being true to himself than most adults are.

I decide to take him to my parents because Mike doesn't get home until 9:00 p.m. that night. He has to go to school in the morning and still works full time. I don't know how he does it.

When I go to my parents, they immediately rush to hold him.

"It's my turn!"

"Let me hold him."

I get a snack from my parents' fridge before his next feeding.

Everywhere I go, it's always the same with Tristan. People can't help but want to hold him. My family, especially, loves taking turns with him while I think about when he needs to eat and when my own next nap should be.

Although I'm glad they love him so much, I'm happy to take him back home.

I settle in on our couch to feed him again as I flip on a show. He eats well this time and before I know it, he's fallen asleep on my chest.

This. This is my favorite place in the world. No, that's not right. This is my favorite *feeling* in the world. Never have I felt such contentment. Everything in the world could be going wrong but when Tristan is on my chest, it feels like things have fallen into place.

As soon as Daddy comes home, Tristan wakes up. No one believes me but I swear he knows when Daddy is home. Mike is such a good dad and immediately takes him from me to play with him and change him.

Tristan loves Daddy. His wide eyes are watching him with that special connection that only fathers and sons have. I wonder if I should be jealous of their strong relationship but I'm not. It fills me with such peace to see them like this.

We're in this 500-square-foot apartment, sleeping on a pull-out bed in the living room so I can watch TV. We don't have a dishwasher or washing machine. But this little family of mine? This is everything.

If I could live for this feeling forever, it would be enough.

After
May 28, 2016 is officially the worst day of my life.

I wake up at 7:20 a.m. It's quiet so I go back to sleep, waiting for Tristan to wake up.

At 7:45 a.m., I wake up to more silence. Something isn't right. He's not breathing.

At 8:15 a.m., we're in the hospital.

At 8:30 a.m., Tristan is declared dead.

At 8:31 a.m., I break.

Is there anything worth living for now?

One Year Later: May 2017
The creature is stirring inside of me.

I close my eyes, feeling the tension growing as the thoughts start to whirl. I've spent the last year battling this creature. It wakes inside of me when I least expect. The creature is ruthless, always spinning my thoughts.

Sometimes I feel it making me angry. Other times it makes me shut down. But most of all, it makes me overthink. I feel trapped in the whirlpool of my own thoughts and feelings.

This creature could be called many things. Anxiety. Post-traumatic stress.

Probably the easiest name is Grief.

I sit up in bed, feeling it rise in me. I'm barely aware of fighting down the tears again as I head out of our bedroom and sit on the couch.

As I close my eyes, I think about the last year I've had.

When it first happened, people called me strong because I wasn't crying all the time. In fact, I was doing fairly well, all things considering. I got a full-time job within three weeks. We moved to a different apartment within a month. I went hiking a lot, trained for a half marathon, spent time with friends and loved ones.

Mike and I even had a chance to go to Chile for two weeks and I saved enough for my dream trip to London.

Ironically, this was everything I wanted before Tristan was born.

So, things obviously weren't all bad. That's something no one told me about Grief.

I could be simultaneously feeling two things at once. I could be having the best day and then it will hit me that I wouldn't be able to travel nearly as much if I still had a baby. Sometimes I'd do a really good job at work and then suddenly need to go home because a memory would trigger anxiety.

I thought about Tristan all the time. I wanted to feel him around me, to feel some sense of purpose, to feel something more. As anniversary dates came up—our first ultrasound, when we found out his gender, the first time I felt him kick—things got hard.

Even with how difficult that is, it's the subtle things that are the hardest.

It's things like sitting with Mike and feeling like something was missing. Then I realized there always will be.

I couldn't laugh at the same things around me. I'd still make friends, but I felt awkward when people would joke about trivial things.

I just felt everything *so* deeply. No matter what I did, I felt it would never leave me.

Someone recommended counseling and it helped slightly, but not completely.

Then I tried just being alone but my thoughts were always spiraling and not always spiraling upward.

I tried doing puzzles. That actually did help. It gave me something to do with my hands, something to work on with Mike.

I wanted to watch TV but I couldn't for months. Everything reminded me of Tristan.

Even church was hard. I prayed and prayed and I wrote pages and pages to work through my grief. I felt comforted, but I also felt profound loneliness.

Then there were the physical changes. I got sick more than ever before. I dropped 15 pounds without meaning to do so, mostly because I couldn't stop moving. People would raise their eyebrows at how much I would walk. When the nights finally came and I was forced to stop moving, that's when the creature would wake up.

I don't know how to describe it. The past year was a blur with happy moments with my husband and family members. I did laugh. There were moments of coming together with Mike. As always, he really was my saving grace.

I also had opportunities to empathize with people and opportunities to travel. Empowering, right? It should have been.

But I kept asking myself—why?

What is this all for? I grip the sides of my head now, feeling myself start to shake. I don't know what I'm living *for*.

I want to live for Tristan, for Mike. I want to live for my future kids. That should be enough, shouldn't it?

I don't know anymore.

End of Summer 2017
I'm running.
Stop thinking, I tell myself. I'm tired.
I'm so sick of this feeling. I want to re-create that meaning I had. I want to be a mom again.
One step. Two steps. Three steps.

Where am I running to? I don't know. Maybe I haven't known in months.

Finally, I stop. I don't even feel winded.

God? You've always answered me before. Please tell me. Tell me why I feel so lost.

I know what it is I'm seeking. Everything about my journey with Tristan, those five weeks he was with me—they were the happiest I've ever been. I want purpose again. I want to understand what I'm living for. I need to know what it is I actually want.

I look at the view before me. I'm in the Grand Canyon. Am I really running along the Havasupai River as though it's nothing?

I don't know what happened inside of me. I've never been a trail runner, but something clicked, and I took off running.

I watch the river. The trees are massive and the sky goes on forever. Is the answer to my questions up there? Maybe Tristan's up there, wishing he could reach me. For the last year, most important to me has been making sure he's remembered.

But now I wonder … maybe there's something more.

I smile up at the stars. I've tried so hard this last year and half to live for my son. But now, I seek clarity. For now, it is enough that I'm living.

Fall 2017

Sometimes I still can't believe how much my life has changed in the last few months.

I wake up early, excited and motivated for class. Not school. Mike has convinced me to do combat sports. Muay Thai and Jiu Jitsu.

WHACK. WHACK. PUNCH.

"Focus on technique!"

Right. Always technique. Honestly? I love it.

I show up for work a few hours later and nearly everyone waves at me as I come in. For the first time in a while, I have a tight-knit group of friends. I start writing.

It was Mike who encouraged me to take the leap. My whole career, I've been in sales or marketing. Now I'm a website copywriter?

I have always wanted to be a writer. Since I was nine, I've told my mom I want to be an author, but I've never acted on it. This part-time website copywriting job seemed like a great way to train myself to write every day. I'm developing the necessary skills to be a professional writer.

The best part is that it's working. Outside of work, I've been writing for at least a couple of hours a day. Words flow from my hands.

Outline, write, rewrite. Brainstorm, write, rewrite.

They're doing a writing contest at work for a short story. I've never won a contest with a cash prize before. Writing's always been my passion, but this would mean so much to me if I could get it right.

I finally think I've gotten this right.

When they tell us they're going to announce the winner at work, it's all I can think about. Even though I'm supposed to be writing website copy for a small business, I can barely focus.

Finally, they announce the winner of each category.

When my name is announced for the category I entered, I just stand there, grinning stupidly.

Everyone is clapping but I feel a bit dazed.

It's happening slowly, but I think I'm starting to live for *something*.

Present

I feel another creature growing inside me.

My eyes open and I sit up and stretch. Instead of overcoming me this time, this creature has me smiling. It drives me to get up, to move. I go about my routine happily.

I read.

I clean.

I work.

I exercise.

This new creature is still with me. This one is called Peace.

I find myself walking, thinking. It used to be that I walked and walked just to get the unimaginable out of my head, never knowing exactly why I was walking. Now I understand that I was trying to find meaning, to find something worth living for.

I don't feel that way now. I'm not even mad about going through the rough times, awful as they were. In fact, some of my most precious memories have come from these last two or three years.

I know where I'm going now.

I stop, sitting at my thinking place. It's a perfect sort of place, set high above the valley I live in. I sit on the bench, looking at the sunrise. I come here often now. Sometimes I just think. Other times I take a book.

Today, though, I have something to say.

"Hi, son," I say to the picture on my phone.

I used to watch his videos every day; I took a walk every day listening to the song that reminded me of him the most. I think I was afraid I'd forget him.

I still watch the videos sometimes, but lately I've taken to just talking to his picture.

"I think I've figured it out," I say, staring at his dark eyes. If I think hard enough I can still imagine how he felt on my chest. I lean back, feeling the lump in my throat start to form. It's a warm day today, despite it being winter, but I'm not complaining.

I wait until the lump settles down. Finally, I speak again.

"I tried to live for you, son. For a while now, I've been telling myself to live for my future kids. To remember that I still have a family and more to come. It's been hard. Sometimes I just try to pass the time."

Am I imagining that warm feeling spreading in my chest?

"Anyway, I figured it out. I will always be living for you, for Daddy, for your future brothers and sisters. I will, son. But Tristan? Today, I finally feel like I'm really living for *me*."

That's it. There are still going to be down days. There'll be up days, too. I'm sure there are many ways to find meaning. Everyone's journey is unique. But I can tell you what mine is about.

Today, I'm living for me.

Aura
Dianne Hardy

I'M FELINE, a smuggled cat, not allowed where I live, Palatial Living. Fancy name for a trailer park, huh? My Mom got me five years ago through a newspaper ad. I came free of charge, didn't cost her one red cent. That made her happy because she's tight, or it might be because she's old—sixty something. Anyway, she rarely talks about money other than to mutter something about it being the root of all evil.

She tries to make me feel guilty when I refuse to eat dry cat food saying, "Don't be ungrateful, Aura. When I was a kid people drowned whole litters of baby cats." I think that's completely off the subject and shouldn't a writer know better? You see, as a baby I was given canned cat food once at my other house and that kind of pleasure stays with you, you know?

Within days of getting me she had me 'fixed.' Ridiculous because being contraband I'm housebound, never been outdoors. I only learned about that sex stuff last summer when she held me up to the window where we watched a couple of cats in the grip of ecstasy. At first it looked interesting; the big orange-striped one clamping down on the black one's head—had her right between his jaws. Just envisioning a fight made my hair stand on end. I was a howling as loud as they were, but safe on my side. Then the mean one quit biting and

131

went to sleep on the other one's back. Much ado about nothing, so I made my way to the computer monitor for a nap. Mom got a real kick out of it, stayed watching until the big one left.

Sleeping's my life. Mom claims I do too much, but she's just jealous because she can't sleep through a night. Needing to pee gets her up and Facebook keeps her up. At three in the morning for Heaven's sake!

She buys stupid toys to intrigue me, like I've forgotten how to play or something. One worked for a short time. A red dot circling the room had me running helter-skelter; until I realized she was controlling the event. That's when I ignored it and between you and me, that was hard.

I'm not your ordinary run-of-the-mill cat. Mom's not ordinary either. We're both gifted…you know, psychically. She says she checked out cats before me and none of them spoke to her soul.

According to her I was crying inconsolably. The kid who was giving me and my siblings away actually tried to dissuade her from choosing me. Pointing, he said, "That one is the smallest, the least ready to wean. She's the runt of the litter."

Mom paid him no attention, simply went with her intuition as usual. As I settled down, nestling comfortably in the palm of her hand, we bonded. On the way home she proclaimed:

I need you, tiny girl.
You smoky ball of fluff
with eyes of karmic bent
to atone my deficit.
You'll be my Aura.

Life hasn't all been rosy. Cats are supposed to be independent. Although embarrassed to admit it, I'm downright needy at times. It's Mom's fault because she's pre-occupied with her music, spending hours at the piano, oblivious to me.

Getting her attention is easier when she talks on the phone and I bite her foot—not hard, just enough to irritate her. She'll yell, "You naughty girl," and toss me across the room. I just haven't found anything to work where music is involved.

Wikipedia says "If you can't beat them join them" means admitting defeat and showing a willingness to work with them. That's what I decided to do with Mom.

I started listening to the music she plays. Much of it is popular stuff from the 1950's—her day, but some is high-brow and technical like the music of Beethoven. To my surprise, I've found I rather like him.

So, when she plays the *Moonlight Sonata,* I come running and sing along. Moonlight does that to me, fence or no fence. *Fur Elise* makes me content enough to fall asleep. Mom doesn't notice whether I'm singing or sleeping because, like I said, at the piano she's in her own world.

That Beethoven must have been one talented guy. He wrote beautiful music when he was deaf—by just hearing it in his head. He sounds rather psychic to me, I think maybe he's one of us.

Besides music, Mom's fanatic about books. They're all over the place, even on our bed. I have to say their attraction escapes me. While okay to lie on, they're not like a box you can climb into and hide. Plus, the content! The stuff she reads can give an ordinary person nightmares—stories by Flannery O'Conner or Stephen King. I've decided all authors are disturbed.

On weekends we get company, Mom's kids—Toni, Rachel, and Glen. They treat me like an interloper, rather than a sister, especially Glen, who makes fun of me. I don't know why. I've never done a thing to him. And the grandkids are the worst, hissing back at me, making faces, pointing, and trying to get at my belly. In defense I once bit one and got shut away in the bedroom. I was punished…not him.

In spite of our trials me and Mom have gotten closer over time. You can tell it by simply looking at me, fat and contented like her, I guess. I used to sleep curled up in a ball, but now I lie stretched out flat, even on my back. She laughs and once said, "You're letting it all hang out, huh Aura?"

As I said, she's psychic like me. She knows when the phone's going to ring and who will be calling. Once she ran to comb her hair and put on lipstick, nearly stepped on me. When I yelled in protest, she said, "Get out of my way, company's coming," and sure enough Ted, our writer friend, showed up a minute later. He always says 'hi' to me before he does her—I love him.

Last summer I had a horrendous encounter with a yellow cat. I sat watching a robin out front when this big guy jumped up on my porch. Viciously, we fought through the screen until Mom, hearing the ruckus, chased the ugly one away. I fled under our bed and stayed for hours. Scheech, I wondered if my tail would ever go back to normal.

Mom often sings to me while we're in our cushy blue chair. It's the place in the house where I have her completely to myself. That's because she and I are the only ones that ever sit in it. Long ago Glen gave the chair a bad rap due to my gray hair pasted here and there.

When he says, "Mom, that chair's loaded with cat hair—you need to vacuum it," she obeys, but his efforts to make me look bad don't work. She and I appreciate the blending of blue and gray because we're sensitive to creative expression—art—which he doesn't understand being Obsessive Compulsive, plus an intolerant redneck.

Anyway, Mom owns hundreds of CDs. My all-time favorite is one of Jim Reeves. We were sitting in our chair listening one day. I was dozing in and out, lulled by the opening strains of *Four Walls*. Jim's caressing voice began: "Out where the bright lights are glowing, you're drawn like a moth to a flame..." I shot up, wide awake. A moth? Where? I'd like to get my paws on that.

Last year a major crisis glued me and Mom fast as a flea on a dog. I've always known when she was leaving—even before she hauled out the suitcase. I'd tried lying on top of it in protest. I'd also hidden, refusing to say good-bye, but neither ever kept her home. She'd only stay away for a short time, a couple of days at the most.

Last September when she left, things felt different. Instead of driving her car she went with Glen, and stayed away. Every few days he'd let himself into our house and call, "Where's my good kitty?" like Mom does. The first time it happened I fell for it and came running—but never again.

Hiding under the bed I thought, Fool me once, shame on you, fool me twice, shame on me. You know I'm pretty smart; I said that better than that one guy—who was he? Oh yeah, Former President George Bush! He was before my time, but Mom must have liked him because she always imitated him in a funny voice and finished with 'heh, heh.'

At our house while Mom was gone, Glen would set out food and fresh water. Then he'd start shoveling crap out of my litter box. Within seconds he'd be cussing like a preacher. Ah, sweet revenge.

Well, the separation wore on both me and Mom. When she came home three weeks later, I was hoarse from crying and wild with fear, not about to let her touch me. Come to think of it, she didn't even try.

She looked scary and wore a big brace on her knee. Even going from our chair to the bathroom, she used her walker and winced with every step. Worse yet, she stared straight ahead all day, no writing, playing the piano—nothing. When the telephone rang, she didn't answer, and Glen had to use his key to get in the house because she wouldn't go to the door.

He'd come in, heat up a can of chicken noodle soup and sit and watch her eat it. That's when I knew for certain something was wrong, because she used to eat all the time, even in the night, and now she didn't want to.

After a week Glen was tired of it; pissed off royally in fact. "All right, Mom, you're going to promise me you won't do anything bad or you have to go live with Rachel so she can watch you. Now which will it be?"

When Mom didn't answer, he yelled, "Either way, your cat will be gone because none of us kids can take her. We already have animals and she won't be able to adapt. You're all she's got."

135

Mom looked over at me, seemed to really notice me for the first time in a long time. I quit licking myself and watched her back. After what felt like an eternity she softly said, "I promise, Glen. I won't do anything bad," and broke down crying.

He softened. "I know it's hard. Losing music must feel like death to you, but the doctors say when the drugs are finally out of your system you might be able to play again. We've got to be patient."

All three kids were at our house the following week.

"Well, Mom, you're looking better than you did when you first had the knee replacement," Toni said. "Sorry, I couldn't stay longer. When I left Roosevelt, it was quiet but just when you came out of surgery, I got a call from my boss saying we had three to embalm, so I had to leave Logan. I said good-bye to you but I doubt you remember it because you were still under the anesthetic. That's the life of a mortician—I'm always on call whether it's slow or they're dying like flies."

I like that. Once I found one, a fly on the window sill—killed and ate it, slicker than shit!

"When did you notice Mom wasn't all right?" Toni asked Glen.

"She was doing well but in a lot of pain while still in the hospital, so they gave her more drugs," he said.

"Yeah," Rachel agreed. "Two days later they took her to a rehab center to recover. She was on massive doses of Morphine, Valium, and Loritab, all at the same time. We were in her room visiting when someone turned on the TV. It was LDS conference and Mom blurted out, "Turn that off. It's a conspiracy."

Toni laughed. "I've never once heard her use that word."

"We hadn't either," Glen chuckled.

"I still feel bad for the help," said Rachel. "The lady on night-shift was sweet and caring, but the more patient she was, the worse Mom treated her—called her Nurse Ratchett in Pink."

"Oh, that's terrible," Toni cried, "Do you think she got it?"

Well, Mom stared straight ahead, but I got it; I'm not called Aura for nothing! I looked over at the video of *One Flew Over the Cuckoo's*

Nest sitting on the bookcase shelf. Mom loves Jack Nicholson because they're both rebels.

"The nurse was probably too young to know the movie." Rachel said. "At any rate, the place got its fill of Mom, said they couldn't deal with her mental condition if it continued. They told us to start looking into lockdown places, didn't they, Glen?"

"Yep. After a couple of days, the doctor reduced her medication, still she was 'out of it' for awhile. The worst was day four when she met her physical therapist. An attendant told her to wait in a large room where there were no chairs. I think he thought she'd use a wheel chair. But Mom went with a walker and finding no chairs, she sat down on the piano bench.

The therapist came in, introduced himself and seeing her at the piano said,

"Do you play?"

"Yes, she said, smiling and placing her hands on the keys. Glen paused. "Evidently she couldn't play a note, and she's been suicidal at different times since. The doctor advised us not to push the music playing. He said Mom would know when the time was right to try. It hasn't happened yet."

So that's it! Here I was thinking the problem was her knee. I should have known it was caused by music and that's why I'd catch her staring at the piano. It also explains the day she hugged me hard enough I had trouble breathing. She cried, "Aura, Aura, help me. Music's been with me longer than anything in my life." All I could do was lick her, so I did that until my tongue was sore.

I guess I should be grateful to her kids for finally giving me answers. Nobody tells a cat anything. Over time Mom began to walk better and her appetite came back. When I heard her humming *Stayin' Alive,* I knew we'd make it. Still, I watched her closely and lay on her lap purring—whole days sometimes.

Her thirteenth day home, I awoke to find her shuffling through movies. She reached for *The Hours.* Knowing I'd better do something drastic, I leapt onto the chair, flew over to the shelf, and knocked

Awakenings to the floor. It's about patients in a hospital for the chronically ill and a doctor who brings them out of a catatonic state.

"Dog-gone-it, Aura. Look what you've done," she yelled, shoving me to the floor. But she picked up the box, thought a moment, and put the movie into the machine. There's a scene where the doctor, Robin Williams, races onto the patients' ward in the middle of the night to find everyone chattering about their lives as though it were forty years before. A man sits at the grand piano playing a Jerome Kern song, *All the Things You Are.*

Mom stared wide-eyed at the TV. Her mouth dropped open. She grabbed the remote and paused the movie. Tossing me from her lap, she rose from our chair and hobbled to the piano.

"I can do that," she declared. Then she played *The Way We Were* as though there'd been no hiatus—laughing and crying at the same time. We didn't even finish the movie.

That was a year ago. Now Glen is having his own crisis. Mom has him come to eat lunch every day because he's depressed and gaunt-looking. I heard her demand that he promise the same thing she promised him—not to do anything bad.

I'm actually getting more used to him. Instead of running to hide when he comes, I stay put on our chair. Mom noticed and told me, "That's good, Aura. You need to be in here with us because we're a family. Maybe you can help him like you did me."

Maybe tragedy changes people. Yesterday he petted me.

The Ride Home
C.H. Hung

The dogs bark at our heels
leaping and twisting in the air
our livelihood delivered for the year

Sunset limns the mountains high
fencing the valleys into open pens
for men and horses to pass on by

The trail is freer than His blessing
no cattle lowing or worries pressing
only a herd of cowboys going home

About the Authors

Originally from South Carolina, **Daniel Cureton** has been living in Utah since 2008. His BA in from the University of Utah in gender studies with minors in Russian lit and Turkish. Daniel has an MLS in archive science from Emporia State University and an MA in English from Weber State University. Daniel considers himself a transgressive and post-modern writer. His poetry exposes the deeper meanings of experiential living and his stories are idea platforms. He has previously been published in *Peculiar: A Queer Literary Journal*, *The Rocky Mountain Review*, *Trilithon: The Journal of the Ancient Order of Druids in America*, A Shanghai Poetry Zine, and *Enheduanna: A Pagan Literary Journal*, for which he is the editor.

Kathy Davidson lives in a small town on the boarders of Bear Lake with her husband and their large hound dog. She went back to school after raising three kids and earned a bachelor's degree in English. She took time out from working on her first novel to write this story for the Idaho Writer's League. Kathy belongs to the Brigham City Chapter and the Just Write Chapter.

Denis Feehan is a writer and musician from Mesquite, NV. He has won several awards from the League of Utah Writers for his poetry and short stories. He is the current president of the Heritage Writer's Guild, a chapter of the LUW in St. George, Utah.

Krystal Gerber did find a mouse living in her bread loaf, but she's quite sure that facing down a grizzly bear with only a stewpot was a worse experience. Both these real-life adventures and many others have given her inspiration for her short stories and novels. In 2018, Krystal won first place in Flash Fiction for the League of Utah Writers as well as Honorable mention. A happily engaged member of the LUW, Krystal lives in northern Utah and will graduate as an English teacher if learning French doesn't kill her first. You can connect with Krystal on Facebook at www.facebook.com/authorKrystalGerber and on Instagram: @authorKrystalGerber

J. Anthony Gohier enjoys all forms of creative writing. He has degrees in media arts and computer science and has found many similarities between them. He has worked on film productions for Discovery Channel and Disney and has also had several short stories and poems published in anthologies and online magazines.

Katharine Goodman is the founder and president of The Red Butte Bards, a poetic chapter in the League of Utah Writers. She has been married to Greg Goodman for 33 years. They share three remarkable children and one fluffy dog named Kona. When she isn't penning poetry, she can be found working on philanthropic efforts with her family through their private foundation, PROVIDE.

A mother of three children and seven grandchildren, **Dianne Hardy** retired in December 2008 after spending the last 46 years in piano teaching—the last 20 in higher education. She loves the slower pace of her life and feels only one compulsion, to create every day. She is the author of her childhood memoir, *For Cryin' Out Loud!*

Joni B. Haws lives in South Jordan with her husband and three kids. She continues to walk the tightrope between faith and doubt, using her family and the feelings in her own heart as a balancing rod. Along with creative non-fiction, she writes horror and urban fantasy. When not writing, Joni can be found creating custom greeting cards, arranging flowers, crocheting, belting power ballads in the shower, directing church choir, or checking inventory in her Little Free Library. Contact at JoniBHaws@gmail.com.

Sariah Horowitz explores the world on digs, in books, and in her writing. She graduated in archaeology but she thinks of herself as Archie Oogly's Ex (Archaeologist) because no one will pay her to play in the dirt. While on her digs, she imagines fantastical situations that could happen with a little magic in the mundane world. She is a member of the League of Utah Writers. Dig up more of her writing at sariahhorowitzwriter.wordpress.com

C.H. Hung grew up among the musty book stacks of public libraries, where she found a lifelong love for good stories and lost 20/20 vision for good. After a brief stint dabbling in reality, C.H. Hung re-entered the world of myth and fantasy to finally put to paper the dreams and stories she's carried in her head since those long-ago days in the library. Read more at www.chhung.com.

Lorraine Jeffery has a bachelor's degree in English, a MLIS in library science, and has managed public libraries in Texas, Ohio and Utah for over twenty years. She has won poetry prizes in state and national contests and published over sixty poems in various publications, including *Clockhouse, Kindred, Calliope, Ibbetson Street,* and *Rockhurst Review.* Her poems have also been printed in anthologies published by Orchard Press, Bacopa Press. League of Utah Writers and others. Her articles have appeared in many publications, including *Focus on the Family, Mature Years, and Exponent II.* She is the mother of ten children (eight adopted) and lives in Utah.

Tim Keller is a former president of the League of Utah Writers and current president of the League's Cache Valley Chapter. The only thing he likes better than reading a good story is telling one. Tim always wanted to try his hand at writing and began work on the Great American Novel. Since then, he's branched out into short prose and essays, and even works on the novel from time to time.

Caryn Larrinaga is an award-winning mystery, horror, and urban fantasy author. Her debut supernatural mystery novel, *Donn's Hill,* was awarded the League of Utah Writers 2017 Silver Quill in the adult novel category and was a 2017 Dragon Award finalist. Her short horror story, "A Friend in Need," was a 2018 League of Utah Writers award winner. She is a Utah native, horror fanatic, and proud pet parent. Visit www.carynlarrinaga.com for free short stories and true tales of haunted places.

Gregory Lemon fell in love with stories when he discovered a book of Greek myths in his school library. He fell in love with reading when he read the Harry Potter and Little House series to his five children—twice—each. He fell in love with writing when he began to write fiction, an escape from the daily emails and technical documents. He is a member of The Infinite Monkeys and Salt City Genre Writers Chapters of the League of Utah Writers. He earned the Distinguished Toastmaster Award as a member of the Precision Speakers Club of Toastmasters International. He lives in the Salt Lake Valley with his family and can be found at WriterGreg.com.

C.H. Lindsay is a writer, poet, housewife, and mother, but not necessarily in that order. While she hasn't worked at a regular job since her kids were tiny, she spent thirty years as an event planner, organizing and running science fiction, fantasy, and horror conventions. She also spent a decade acting in musicals. Now she prefers to stay home with her family, writing novels, short stories, and poetry. She runs a fleet of online text-based roleplaying simulations. Mostly blind due to a degenerative eye disease, she collects print books for her library and audiobooks for herself. She is a member of SFWA, HWA, SFPA, and LUW. She is a founding member of the Utah Chapter of the Horror Writers Association. She lives in Utah with her "seeing-eye husband," youngest son, and a cat who also considers itself to be a child.

Keri Montgomery writes mainly middle grade and adult speculative fiction. She's a contributing author to *Rise Above Depression*, the former #1 Amazon bestseller in self-help by main author and inspirational speaker Jodi Orgill Brown. Keri's short fiction can be found in the 2019 Utah Horror Writers Anthology *Peaks of Madness*, in the 2018 LUW Press anthology *At First Glance*, and also in the 2019 Brigham City Writers anthology *Spirals*. She's a board member for the League of Utah Writers and founder of the Brigham City Writers chapter. When not writing, she enjoys firefighting with her department, convincing her kids that museums are cool, and wishing for superhuman skills.

David Rodeback lives in American Fork, Utah. A former speech writer, university instructor, and computer programmer, he now works in digital marketing and moonlights as a freelance writer and editor. He once spent the Fourth of July in the Soviet Union, being interrogated by the Moscow Police and scowled at by the KGB.

Felicia Rose's work has appeared in *The Dandelion Review, The Helicon West Anthology, The Sun, The Way to My Heart: An Anthology of Food-Related Romance, Mother Earth News,* and elsewhere. Her short story "Jofi" will be published in the upcoming issue of *The Westchester Review*. A native New Yorker, she makes her home in Cache Valley, Utah.

Samantha Thorup is a multi-award-winning author. Having fallen in love with writing at the age of 9, she always knew she wanted to be an author. She wrote this piece for her son, Tristan Thorup, who passed away from SIDs at 5 weeks old. The 3 T's are important to her: traveling, tacos, and time with family.

Marie Tollstrup taught for thirty-nine years. At Jordan High School in North Long Beach, she founded and advised *Stylus*, a national award-winning literary/arts magazine for twenty-three years. In retirement, Marie focuses on poetry, but branches out to articles, short stories, and creative non-fiction which she enters into local, state, and national contests, winning awards for speaking her mind and poetic word play.

Pam Tucker's poetry has appeared in *Trestle Creek Review, Plainsongs, Literary Mama,* and *Prairie Poetry.* Her collection of poems *Topography of Light* won honorable mention in the poetry division of the 2018 Utah Original Writing Competition. She is the author of the children's book *Paper Monsters* illustrated by Mark Ludy. Pam received a BA in English from BYU. Growing up in small town Wyoming gave her a love for big sky and wide open spaces. She loves hitting the road on a bicycle with a map, granola bar and an empty schedule. She lives in Washington, UT.

E.B. Wheeler attended BYU, majoring in history with an English minor, and earned graduate degrees in history and landscape architecture from Utah State University. She's the author of seven novels, including Whitney Award finalist *Born to Treason* and *Utah Women: Pioneers, Poets, and Politicians* (November 2019 from The History Press), as well as several short stories, magazine articles, and scripts for educational software programs. The League of Utah Writers named her the 2016 Writer of the Year. In addition to writing, she consults about historic preservation and teaches history at USU. You can find her online at ebwheeer.com

www.ingramcontent.com/pod-product-compliance
Lightning Source LLC
Chambersburg PA
CBHW071347170626
46811CB00003B/1027